# How to Break Into Pharmaceutical Sales

## *A Headhunter's Strategy*

### by

# Tom Ruff

Waverly
Press

New York

# Acclaim for Tom Ruff's
## *How to Break Into Pharmaceutical Sales*
### *A Headhunter's Strategy*

Best Books Award **FINALIST!** USA Book News

"With Tom Ruff, the glass of opportunity is never half-full. It's always brimming over. So if you're interested in sales, this step-by-step book will help you channel your energies to succeed. Not just in selling a product, but in selling yourself."

— John Pollack, former presidential speechwriter and author of *Cork Boat*

"The book, published by Waverly Press, is straightforward, giving the reader tips on résumés, networking and interviews, among other topics."

— *South Bend Tribune*, June 2007

"Without a proper road map, a candidate can waste years searching for work in this competitive industry. Tom Ruff has provided such a road map: succinct, informative, practical. It should be required reading for anybody seeking a position in pharmaceutical sales."

— Michael Olson, President, Highland Search Executive Recruiting

"*How to Break Into Pharmaceutical Sales* teaches you to make the most important sale you could ever make — yourself. After that, the products and services you are selling will follow. A great book!"

— Steve Johnson, President and CEO of The Next Level Sales Consulting
author of *Selling Is Everyone's Business*

"Tom Ruff knows the ins and outs of the pharmaceutical sales industry. He knows what it takes not only to break in, but how to thrive once you're there. Now he's put all of his secrets in one place. If you want to learn from a master, do not miss Tom's book."

— Rob Heidger, Sales Representative of the Year, Mentor Corporation
United States Olympic Beach Volleyball Player 2000

"This is a great book. Tom Ruff knows better than anyone how to prepare you to break into this challenging field. Follow his directions in this book, and you will blow your competition away."

— Ken MacDonald, Regional Sales Manager (Retired), Abbott Laboratories

"Tom Ruff is a coach's coach. His book is the definitive guide to breaking into the pharmaceutical sales field. He will prepare you not only to win, but to emerge a champion."

— Jim Connelly, Chairman, Integrated Communications Services
motivational speaker and author of *One More Sunset*

# What Job-Seekers Are Saying...

"I definitely recommend *How to Break into Pharmaceutical Sales* for those trying to break into the industry. It became my bible in the job search. A few months after reading the book, I received a job offer from Bristol-Myers Squibb!"

— **Kimberly Hoffman, Chicago, Illinois**

"This is the best book on the topic. I've read Anne Clayton's book, it was recommended to me as one of the best resources in the field, but I think Ruff's book is even better! It has great hands-on tips, lots of data and statistics about the field, excellent direct feedback from people working in the field, is easy to read and scan through, and is super-motivational."

— **Kerry Newman, Philadelphia, Pennsylvania**

"I read this book and it worked! I accepted an offer from Roche Pharmaceuticals this morning! I really think that the advice offered is what put me ahead of the other candidates. I can't stress enough how much I loved the book."

— **Tiffany Austin, Monroe, North Carolina**

"This book is a must have for anyone trying to enter the pharmaceutical sales field, especially for someone who has no outside sales experience. It lays out exactly what must be done to make yourself stand out. I would recommend reading *How to Break Into Pharmaceutical Sales* before going any further in your pursuit of a pharmaceutical sales career. I feel that anyone who reads this book and follows Tom's advice closely will be able to land the job they desire."

— **Jamie Eshleman, Santa Rosa, California**

"...One of the deciding factors in choosing me as their candidate was that I "closed the deal", a technique that was emphasized in Tom Ruff's book. They told me that I was the only candidate that actually asked for the job."

— **Patti Purser, Hattiesburg, Mississippi**

"This book completely changed the way I am approaching a career in pharmaceutical sales. I have a panel interview coming up next week with a very well known pharmaceutical company and have been extremely nervous, but your tips (especially the panel interview section) helped give me the confidence I need to go into that interview and make sure I nail it."

— **Emily Regensburg, King of Prussia, Pennsylvania**

"Tom covers everything about what to expect, what to know, and how to research and prepare, right down to the last detail! After reading it, I cannot imagine how anyone could compete in the interviewing process without knowing and doing these things."

— **Becky Garza, Napa, California**

This publication has been designed to provide competent and reliable information regarding the subject matter covered. However, it is sold with the understanding that the author and publisher are not engaged in rendering legal, financial or other professional advice. Laws and practices often vary from state to state and if legal or other expert assistance is required, the services of a professional should be sought. The author and publisher specifically disclaim any liability that is incurred from the use or application of the contents of this book. The purchase of this book does not guarantee employment in the pharmaceutical industry.

ISBN-10: 0-9786070-1-5
ISBN-13: 978-0-9786070-1-2

Publisher's Cataloging-in-publication
(Provided by Quality Books, Inc.)

Ruff, Tom.
    How to break into pharmaceutical sales : a
    headhunter's strategy / by Tom Ruff.
    p. cm.
    Includes index.

    1. Selling—Drugs—Vocational guidance.  2. Drugs—
    Marketing—Vocational guidance.  3. Pharmaceutical
    industry—Management—Vocational guidance.  I. Title.

    HF5439.D75R84 2007    615'.10688    QBI07-600014

Printed in the USA
First Edition
First printing June 2007
Second printing September 2007
Third printing February 2008

10,9,8,7,6,5,4,3

Waverly Press books are available at special quantity discounts to use as premiums or for special programs, including corporate training. Book excerpts can also be created to fit specific needs.

For information please e-mail customorder@waverlypress.com or write to Waverly Press, Rockefeller Center, 1230 Avenue of the Americas, 7th Floor, New York, NY 10020. You can visit us on the Web: www.waverlypress.com.

# This book is dedicated to

*My guiding light, my rock and the first person who inspired
me to lead a life of integrity, faith and good will
— my mother, Phyllis A. Woolsey*

*The loving memory of my mentor, my constant teacher
and my best friend
— my father, Dr. Eldon E. Ruff*

# INTRODUCTION

" Whatever you can do or dream you can, begin it. Boldness has genius, power and magic in it. "

— GOETHE

Y ou could say I became an entrepreneur at the age of eight. That summer Mrs. Bond asked me to mow her lawn. When she paid me $8, I thought I was the richest kid in the world. The lawn-mowing business my neighbor helped me start sustained me all the way through college — along with my snow-plowing business, car-detailing operation and, eventually, t-shirt company. After I graduated from Indiana University, I moved to Chicago and lived in the basement of my friend's mother's home with a $99 suit, a pair of wing tip dress shoes, my shoe-shine kit and a stack of books, including *Think and Grow Rich* by Napoleon Hill, *The Power of Positive Thinking* by Norman Vincent Peale and *How to Win Friends and Influence People* by Dale Carnegie. I didn't know what I was going to do, but I knew that, at some point, I would own my own company. For my first job, I went to work for one of the top sales recruiting firms in the country, SalesSource, based in Chicago. Within a year, I was the company's number one recruiter, a distinction I held in my second year as well. In my third year, I headed west to oversee the successful launch of the company's Los Angeles office.

Several months later, I took the plunge. I struck out and opened a recruiting firm of my own. I remember how hard it was trying to recruit people to go on interviews with car rental or telephone companies. One day a man named Andy, who would become a close friend, walked into my office. He worked for one of the country's largest and most respected pharmaceutical companies. He and his colleagues wore sharp navy suits and bright white shirts. My candidates did not need convincing to interview for the positions Andy was trying to fill. People lined up at the door for a chance to speak with him. One hopeful candidate brought me a bottle of wine. Another brought a gift basket. A light bulb went off in my head — and from that point on I began to focus exclusively on placing people in pharmaceutical sales positions.

Our business has grown dramatically since then and we are now a preferred recruiter for 100 of the country's top pharmaceutical and medical device companies. People seek careers in pharmaceutical sales for a number of powerful, practical reasons, which you will read more about in Chapter One; it's no surprise that in 2007 CNNMoney.com selected it as one of The 20 Best Jobs in America. For starters, the pay is high and the field prestigious. Pharmaceutical sales representatives use their selling skills to educate doctors and pharmacists about new and important drug therapies. As such, they play a key role in the advancement of medicine and must communicate effectively with an exceptionally educated customer. The benefits packages in pharmaceutical sales are, quite simply, without equal. Undeniably these attributes draw many new sales people to the field. But there's another reason, too: pharmaceutical sales representatives play a crucial part in helping people to live healthier, longer lives.

If you follow even half of the tips outlined in this book, you will stand out among the thousands of other job-seekers. In 18 years of placing candidates in jobs as pharmaceutical sales representatives — often through exclusive contracts with the country's largest pharmaceutical companies — I've discovered sure-fire strategies for finding work in this exciting field. My goal is to show you the fastest and most effective means of breaking in.

---

Tom Ruff Company has conducted proprietary research into the key factors in obtaining work in pharmaceutical sales. More than 150 pharmaceutical sales representatives participated. Some 20 district managers for major pharmaceutical companies answered a separate set of questions. All were guaranteed confidentiality. The results of this survey, with verbatim responses, are excerpted in the book and collected in Chapter 15.

**For more information about Tom Ruff Company, visit www.tomruff.com.**

# CONTENTS

# The Job

A pharmaceutical representative markets prescription medications to, and acts as an educational liaison for, physicians, pharmacies and hospitals. As a pharmaceutical sales representative, your primary objective is to persuade a physician to prescribe your products for appropriate patients, based on need and clinical studies.

# A Career Path in Pharmaceutical Sales

Sales Representative
↓
Senior Sales Representative
↓
Field Sales Trainer
↓
Hospital Sales Representative or Specialty Sales Representative
↓
District Manager
↓
Managed Care Executive or Product Manager or 1-year, "in-house" rotation position
↓
Regional Director
↓
Area Director
↓
Vice President of Sales
↓
President of Sales

*Career paths vary from company to company.*

## CHAPTER ONE

# Why Pharmaceutical Sales?

**❝** I have always been delighted at the prospect of a new day, a
fresh try, one more start, with perhaps a bit of magic
waiting somewhere behind the morning. **❞**

**– J. B. Priestly**

L ou, one of my best friends, wasn't always happy in sales. Years ago, he made a living selling products he found dull and uninteresting. "I hated it, and I wasn't good at it," he says. "It weighed on my mental state."

Needing a change, Lou parlayed his experience into a new career in pharmaceutical sales. He began selling a popular asthma drug in urban areas where many kids went untreated. One day he called on a doctor there who listened to Lou's pitch. Though skeptical, the doctor began prescribing the medication. A few months later, on a return visit, that same doctor ushered Lou into his office and showed him a basket brimming with homemade breads and jams. One of his patients was a little boy who had suffered from severe unrelieved asthma. The medicine Lou sold improved the child's quality of life so dramatically that his mother sent the gift basket to the doctor as a thank-you. Lou was surprised to find himself heading out to his car with tears in his eyes.

"I like that better than my bonus check," he says. "When you hear how somebody benefited from a drug and how it changed a life, it makes you feel good and you sleep a little better at night."

Pharmaceutical companies and their sales representatives, especially the passionate ones like Lou, play a dynamic role in helping people better navigate both illness and the inevitable onset of infirmity. A sobering fact of life is that disease and old age are unavoidable. No matter what the state of the economy, people will always need medicines to cure them and appropriate drugs to maintain their health.

Make no mistake, the goal of every effective pharmaceutical sales representative is to sell their companies' new and pre-existing drug therapies. Pharmaceutical companies pay them well for this service, giving the profession cachet and appeal; many starting representatives make an average of $100,000 a year in salary and benefits. Along the way, however, they are educating doctors, dentists and pharmacists about the pros and cons of new medicines, the method of prescription, the ideal patient population and many other associated matters. Another good friend, Keri Oberg, a pharmaceutical sales representative in Los Angeles, has found a life's calling making a concrete difference in the lives of people living with HIV, both at home and through her travels in Africa. Representatives like Keri and Lou all over the world, covering different diseases and therapeutic categories, keep doctors informed and do what they can to ensure patients have access to new, cutting-edge treatments.

That is especially important to members of the Boomer population, now entering retirement age, who are not ones to fade off passively into the sunset. They are aggressively seeking treatments and cures for everything that ails them. As this population continues to mature, the demand for constantly improving remedies will continue to grow. The size of this aging demographic continues to drive growth in the industry.

While there were only 20,000 pharmaceutical sales representatives working in the United States in 1970, that number has jumped to an estimated 100,000 today, according to Bob Davenport, vice-president of the consultancy Hay Group, which regularly surveys the industry. Word-of-mouth from this group's family members, friends and acquaintances is driving an ever-increasing number of job hunters to follow in their footsteps. Based on the number of résumés flowing into pharmaceutical companies, many times that number of people are searching for work in the field at any given time. While the number of working representatives has doubled in the past five years, the size of the work force now appears to be stabilizing. The result is an increasingly competitive job market. Candidates looking to break in need all the help they can get.

For those who succeed, it's worth the effort. The economics behind this profession are impressive. Research and development investments in new medicines by the biopharmaceutical industry totaled more than $55 billion in 2006, an 8% increase over 2005, according to a combined analysis conducted by Burrill & Company and the Pharmaceutical Research and Manufacturers of America (PhRMA). Globally, total sales for the pharmaceutical industry stood at $582 billion in 2006, representing 6.2% growth over the previous year, according to Standard & Poor's. If numbers alone aren't sufficiently persuasive, consider a recent Hay Group survey published in *Pharmaceutical Representative* magazine. The survey found that pharmaceutical company employees report higher levels of job satisfaction than their counterparts in other industries. Nearly nine out of ten interviewed expressed pride in their company and 95% had favorable attitudes toward their companies' products and services.

The high employee satisfaction may also be due to the fact that a career in pharmaceutical sales confers prestige not only due to its high compensation, but as an acknowledgment of the brainpower it requires. Pharmaceutical representatives meet with an exceptionally highly educated customer. Doctors and pharmacists aren't pushovers. You can't be either.

Few outsiders realize that pharmaceutical companies invest more than almost any other industry in training their sales representative — almost $100,000 a person.

My friend Lou once worked in a sales job where clients could intimidate him because he was ill-prepared to take on their questions. He often found himself saying, "I don't have the answer. Let me get back to you on that." This quickly changed when he went to work for a large pharmaceutical company.

"The first day I started the job," Lou says, "one of my new colleagues said to me, 'So, I hear you're off to med school.' I laughed, but then noticed that no one else did. I thought that was a little odd."

Soon Lou understood that "going to med school" as a sales representative was serious business. His employer put him through the paces. He studied the biology and pharmacology behind his products so thoroughly that now, when he goes out on sales calls, he's eager to take on the doctors' tough questions.

To this day, he finds the work engaging and mentally stimulating. If you think you will be bored or put off by the effort required to master a new field of study, then working as a pharmaceutical sales representative isn't for you. But if you require mental stimulation to enjoy your profession, you stand to enjoy a long and rewarding career in the field.

*Pharmaceutical companies invest an average of $100,000 in training for each of their sales representatives.*

According to Salary.com, the median salary, including benefits, for a pharmaceutical sales representative nationwide is $95,660. In Chicago, that number is $103,688, in Los Angeles $108,227 and in New York $113,114. You'll also have the chance to work out of your home office and, in some cases, to work flexible hours.

## Here are some other key basics:

### BASE COMPENSATION:

- 0-2 years of industry experience: $42,000 - $50,000
- 2-5 years of non-industry outside sales experience: $50,000 - $58,000
- 2-5 years of industry experience: $58,000 - $65,000
- 5+ years of industry experience: $65,000 - $75,000

### BONUS:

- Average Bonus: $15,000 - $20,000
- Experienced Bonus: $18,000 - $30,000
  (Anyone with more than two to three years of outside sales experience)

### A PARTIAL LIST OF BENEFITS:

- An average of three weeks of vacation in the first year
- Company car, including all gas, comprehensive insurance, all maintenance, from oil changes to tire replacements, and a per diem for personal gas use, valued at $7,000 to $8,000 a year
- Health insurance: full coverage for primary healthcare, dental, vision, spouse, pregnancy and birth, and children
- Equipment, including laptop and cell phone or cell phone reimbursement
- Most home office expenses

- All business expenses
- 401k includes employer match
- Stock option purchase plan, activated at date of tenure in some cases
- Full tuition reimbursement
- Spouse and children benefits
- Daycare service discounts

If these benefits sound too good to be true, don't take my word for it. Go to this link on the Web, and check out Pfizer's extraordinarily comprehensive plan, with 34 bullet-point categories. http://pfizer.com/pfizer/are/careers/mn_working_benefits.jsp

# Education and Background

Many prospective job candidates worry that they don't have the medical or technical background to secure a position. While such preparation is a plus, it is by no means an absolute requirement. A person with the intelligence and will to master the complex, multi-syllabic language of the pharmaceutical world, combined with a winning sales-oriented personality, will be highly prized — even if his or her degree is in English or Religious Studies.

## PREFERRED BACKGROUND:

- Four-year Bachelor's Degree with an emphasis on science
- 3.0 Cumulative GPA or higher
- Ideally, 2+ years of Fortune 500 outside sales experience
- Clean driving record, good credit and no bankruptcies

## ACCEPTABLE BACKGROUND:

- Four-year Bachelor's Degree
- 2.5 GPA or higher
- No more than two traffic tickets in the last six years is a general rule of thumb

## TOTAL COMPENSATION
(base + bonuses + benefits)

| BENEFIT | MEDIAN AMOUNT | % OF TOTAL |
|---|---|---|
| Base Salary | $53,897 | 56% |
| Bonuses | $16,697 | 17% |
| Social Security | $5,400 | 6% |
| 401k/403b | $2,555 | 3% |
| Disability | $1,722 | 2% |
| Healthcare | $5,390 | 6% |
| Pension | $2,287 | 2% |
| Time Off | $7,711 | 8% |
| **TOTAL** | **$95,660** | **100%** |

*Source: Salary.com*

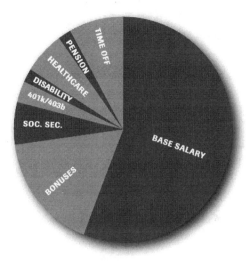

# KNOCKOUT FACTORS:

- No 4-year degree
- A DWI or a DUI
- Bankruptcy within last three to five years
- More than three traffic tickets in last five years
- Criminal Record
- Bad credit
- Failed drug test

In addition, people of all ages and backgrounds qualify to become sales representatives. Although it can be difficult, some enter the profession right out of college and/or without any prior outside sales experience. Pharmaceutical companies also realize that different doctors may respond as well or even more readily to someone who is mature and seasoned. Recently, pharmaceutical companies have increased the number of nurses they hire into the field. If you have a background in nursing, you have a particular advantage. However, not having the classic educational or experiential background need not be a hindrance — as long as you're willing to throw yourself into the pursuit of the job.

While it is up to you to supply passion, focus and commitment, I will empower you with the most effective tools to make your dream come true.

## CHAPTER TWO

# How It's Done

**❝** A goal is a dream with a deadline. **❞**

— **Napoleon Hill**

*The story of how an entry level candidate, without any outside sales experience, lands a job with the largest and most respected pharmaceutical company in the world*

One day a few years back, I got a call from a young woman who wanted us to find her a job in pharmaceutical sales. By the time I put down the receiver I knew, beyond a shadow of a doubt, that she would succeed. Yet, she didn't have any outside sales experience — and she was a recent college graduate. What set her apart? Four things: an extraordinary drive, an unshakable self-confidence, a willingness to listen to everything I told her down to each detail and a resolve to take action. She was so eager to learn. To this day, I still remember the conviction in her voice. She asked questions. She was serious. She was determined.

Among many other things, I told her to go to her doctor's office and request copies of the business cards that pharmaceutical sales representatives leave. Then, I told her to go to a hospital and talk directly to the representatives themselves as they worked their daily beats. In their blue or black suits and rolling briefcases, they are unmistakable. "Be polite, be solicitous and give them your résumé," I said. "You can do that?" she asked me. Yes, I told her, she could. (I emphasized that she needed to let the representatives know she was on a job hunt, so they would not mistake her for an undercover investigator from the FDA). It's such simple advice, but few people take it. Before we hung up, she thanked me profusely and told me she would call me *when* she broke in.

Three months later, I heard her voice again when I picked up the phone. With great excitement, she told me how she had spent the better part of a day standing in front of Cedars Sinai, a large and prominent hospital in West Los Angeles. She approached pharmaceutical sales representatives and handed them her résumé, asked for their business cards and talked up those who had the time and inclination to talk about their careers.

She then proceeded to follow up with each of them. She impressed one of them sufficiently that he told his manager about this young woman. The manager had never heard of anyone going to such lengths. He loved this vivid account of her drive, initiative and good-spiritedness — all important attributes for success in the field. He called her in for an interview. Not having any opening to fill in that moment, he passed her résumé on to another district manager in a different division. After only several months of devoted work — including plenty of rejection along the way — this recent college graduate ended up with a job working in Palm Springs, California, for Pfizer, one of the largest and most respected pharmaceutical companies out there. "Tom!" she yelled, "I GOT THE JOB!"

Without the requisite experience, everyone told her it couldn't be done. She proved them wrong. And so can you! That was more than a decade ago. The field has become exponentially more competitive in the intervening years. Now, when hopeful candidates like this young woman call me, I've got a book's worth of strategies to share. Breaking in is a far more challenging task. While working with the right recruiter can give you a distinct advantage, it is still possible to secure a position on your own using the strategies I will share with you. But one thing is still true. This candidate from so many years ago illustrates the fact that a burning desire is as important as anything else you've got on your résumé — if not more so.

So, let me ask you a few questions. Are you willing to send out hundreds of résumés, to scour the Internet for data, to attend industry trade shows and job fairs and to network with anyone who will listen (and even those who won't), whether they are doctors, pharmacists, receptionists or your cousin's cousin's cousin?

If the answer is no, do yourself a favor and close this book. This field is too crowded if you're not committed. It will get discouraging at times. You may indeed feel you want to give up. But persistence will carry the day.

As the legendary football coach Vince Lombardi said, "To achieve success, whatever the job we have, we must pay a price."

If you are committed, then you're ready to start. Let's get to work.

## Develop a game plan for finding your dream job — and write it down

Using a notebook, a sheet of paper, your Palm Pilot or your computer, find a place to write down your personal plan of action, outlining how you will find a job in pharmaceutical sales. I am going to give you many strategies in this book. Take the ones that you feel are most important to you and write them down. Refer to them daily — even twice daily — and refine the list as you go. Just the act of writing down your goals generates an alchemy that will help you in the hunt. In my own life, I've found over and over that setting goals works. By making a commitment in your own hand and in your own words, you take ownership of the project. Only you can make it happen.

Here are a few questions to get you started:

1) What is your target date for finding a pharmaceutical sales job?
2) How many résumés are you going to send out on a weekly basis?
3) How many new contacts are you going to make on a daily basis? On a weekly basis?
4) How many doctors' offices will you visit to get names and business cards of the sales representatives who call on them?
5) How many pharmacies are you going to call on this week to get the names and business cards of the sales representatives who call on them?
6) How many hospitals will you stand in front of this month waiting for sales representatives to walk by and collect business cards and hand out résumés?
7) How many job fairs will you attend this month?
8) How many pharmaceutical industry trade shows?
9) How many pharmaceutical networking events?
10) How many calls will you make and/or how many emails will you send this week to friends, neighbors, colleagues and to the network you've developed to solicit names of people who work in the industry?

Take the time to seriously contemplate and answer these questions. You will be amazed at how quickly new opportunities present themselves as soon as you do. The action of writing out your goals alone will get the power of your subconscious mind working for you. Soon you will be getting your name and qualifications in front of dozens of people who can help you in your search. Before you actually pick up a phone or meet anyone in person though, you've got to undertake some critical and unavoidable preparations. That is the subject of the next two chapters.

## TOM'S TIP – GOAL SETTING

I'M A FIRM BELIEVER IN THE POWER OF SETTING GOALS. When I look back on some of the most significant things I've accomplished in my lifetime, I realize that the majority of them began with clearly defined, written goals, structured around a specific timeline with benchmarks along the way.

I SET GOALS FOR EVERYTHING I DO, both personally and professionally. Doing so forces me to clarify what I want to accomplish and by when. The simple act of writing down your goals engages your subconscious, which goes to work for you even while you sleep.

AT THE SAME TIME I WRITE DOWN THOSE GOALS, I decide how I will reward myself when I hit them. Some of the smaller rewards have included: taking an afternoon off and going to a movie, going out to a nice dinner, buying something that I've wanted for a long time or going to an amusement park. For some of the bigger or annual goals, I've taken trips to the British Virgin Islands, Fiji, France, Italy and Spain. It's important to have some fun with this.

I ALSO USE VISUALIZATION. I paste color photos of my reward all around my written goals, displaying them in my office. It's nice to come into my office early in the morning and see my goals festooned with these enticing images. It provides a fun way to focus my energy, prioritize my time and accomplish what I want to, when I want to.

## CHAPTER THREE

# Résumé and Brag Book

**"** By failing to prepare, you are preparing to fail. **"**

— Benjamin Franklin

# The Résumé

There are two things you need before you begin your hunt — a résumé and a brag book. First, the résumé: we receive hundreds of résumés on a weekly basis and the average time we spend looking at each one is three to five seconds. In other words, like the pharmaceutical companies themselves, we make a lot of split-second decisions. It's your job to put together a résumé that will tell us your essential story in that short window of time or convince us to spend more time looking at what you've written.

Based on 18 years of recruiting experience and interviews with hundreds of district managers, we have concluded that one of the three following basic résumés works best for prospective pharmaceutical sales representatives. Copy them exactly. It's what we use for all our candidates.

The first one is geared to what I'll call the "underdog" candidate, possibly someone who is just out of college, with limited experience.

# YOUR NAME

Address
City, State Zip
Phone
Email

## OBJECTIVE

Seeking a pharmaceutical sales representative position within a growth-oriented company where advancement and earnings are based upon performance and achievement.

## EXPERIENCE

**Xerox Corporation**                              **Chicago, IL**
**Sales Intern**                          **June 2005–Present**
Responsible for qualifying daily sales leads and achieving activity targets.
- Maintained organization to provide efficient operations.
- Focused on customer satisfaction and detail.
- Consistently performed over 100% of quota.

**U.S. Department of Commerce**              **Chicago, IL**
**International Division**          **January 2005–June 2005**
**Intern**
Conducted market research for companies interested in expanding internationally. Represented the USDOC at trade shows and assisted with client counseling.

## EDUCATION

**Northwestern University**                       **Chicago, IL**
                                                    **June 2005**
- Bachelor of Arts, Sociology

## ATHLETIC ACHIEVEMENTS

- Member of Northwestern University Basketball and Track and Field Teams                                 **2002–2005**
- Captain of Basketball Team — All-American Honors
                                                  **2004–2005**

*For the candidate who comes with strong skills, but no experience in sales, here is an actual résumé for one of our candidates who did indeed find work in the field.*

# YOUR NAME

Address
City, State Zip
Phone
Email

## OBJECTIVE

Seeking a pharmaceutical sales representative position within a growth-oriented company where advancement and earnings are based upon performance and achievement.

## EXPERIENCE

**Physical Education and Health Teacher**          **Contra Costa County, CA**
                                    **2003–Present**

- Planned and coordinated lesson plans for school children aligned with the California Standards for Education.
- Assessed and monitored student progress along with calculating grades and preparing report cards.
- Coordinated after-school sports for middle school children.
- Supervised 20 coaches, 18 sports teams and over 350 student athletes.
- Recruited and monitored coaches, planned and scheduled games, practices and referees, and processed payroll.
- Networked with principal, coaching staff, parents and other athletic directors to maintain communication and ensure an effective program.

**California State University, Chico**          **Chico, CA**
**Program Coordinator**          **August 2002–June 2003**

- Designed and implemented CSU-sponsored programs for adults and children with disabilities.
- Recruited clients from the community, designed personal fitness plans for clients, monitored and documented client

progress, coordinated over 40 volunteers, equipment and facilities.
- Increased number of clients in program and volunteers.

## EDUCATION

**University of California, Chico**                    **May 2004**
- Master of Arts, Physical Education GPA: 3.8
- Bachelor of Arts, Physical Education, Teacher Education GPA: 3.6

---

*For the more experienced candidate, we use the following format.*

# YOUR NAME

Address
City, State Zip
Phone
Email

## OBJECTIVE

Seeking a pharmaceutical sales representative position within a growth-oriented company where advancement and earnings are based upon performance and achievement.

## EXPERIENCE

**Xerox Corporation,**                    **Los Angeles, CA**
**Major Account Executive**              **June 2001–Present**
**Sales Representative**
- #1 Sales Representative 2004 – 10 out of 12 months
- #1 Sales Representative Producer in Los Angeles Office 2005 YTD
- Ranked in the top 15 Sales Representatives Nationwide 2005 YTD
- Certificate of achievement award May 2002 – 200% over quota
- Responsible for obtaining one of the largest accounts nationwide – The County of Los Angeles

- Highest Net Revenue Award October 2004 — 675% over quota
- Circle of Excellence Award — 2001 and 2004
- Surpassed expected quota 2001–2002 — 200%
- Promoted to Major Account Executive after 9 Months

**Gallo Wine Company**        **Los Angeles, CA**
**Sales Representative**        **May 1999–June 2001**
- Top Closer 2000–2001
- Increased revenue 30%
- Sales Representative of the Month Award

## EDUCATION

**University of California, Los Angeles**        **May 1999**
- Bachelor of Arts, Communication
- Graduated Summa Cum Laude

## ATHLETIC ACHIEVEMENTS

- Member of University of California, Los Angeles Football and Track and Field Teams 1995–1999
- Captain of Football, 1998-1999/Captain of Track and Field, 1997–1999 (All-American Honors)
- UCLA Senior Scholar

---

Short and sweet is the name of the résumé game. District managers, who make the key hiring decisions in most pharmaceutical companies, don't want long essays. They simply don't have the time for them. We've found that the main thing that "pops" on a résumé is a bullet-point format loaded with great numbers. For example: "130% of quota, ranked #1 out of 75 sales representatives for 2004, 180% growth in territory," etc. A brief industry objective focused on pharmaceutical sales, company name, title, dates, results and education at the bottom, combined with relevant extra curriculars, rounds out your presentation.

If you played collegiate athletics, or served in the military, make sure to add this to the bottom of your résumé.

Over and over again, district managers will ask us whether or not a prospect played athletics in college. This can be a deciding factor, especially if you lack optimal educational or work experience. We always instruct our candidates to add their athletic experience, even if they've been out of college for five to ten years. Often, they are surprised to think this could be relevant, but it is. The reason is this: playing college athletics requires the ability to work on a team and the ability to motivate yourself to excel. Military experience demonstrates the same qualities. A candidate's background with any branch of the military or national guard will be highly prized by pharmaceutical companies, especially particular ones, like Pfizer.

If you didn't play college athletics, there are a number of other activities worthy of mention. We've told candidates to mention a black belt in Tae Kwon Do, a Toastmasters' public speaking award or a particularly impressive musical accomplishment. One of our candidates came to us with a résumé that wasn't remarkable. However, he was a competitive triathlete. Sharon, one of our team members at Tom Ruff Company, competes regularly in Hawaii's legendary Iron Man. She felt an instant kinship with this candidate because of their shared interest. On that basis alone, we brought him in. Like pharmaceutical companies, we understand the tremendous determination it requires to compete in triathalons. We gave him some simple coaching. He latched on to all our advice and put it to work. Very quickly he got a job — beating out candidates with far more impressive-looking résumés. He had moved to California from Hawaii to break into the field (now that's dedication!). His new employer was so happy with his work that, less than a year later, they moved him back to Hawaii to work for the company.

Any accomplishment you have that demonstrates the mastery of a difficult skill — physical or mental — or the achievement of an impressive benchmark or award may be worth including on your résumé. The point is, if you've got it, brag about it! The résumé is no place to be humble. Your competitors will use everything they have. So should you.

One piece of advice: be careful if you use a résumé-writing service. Often our candidates turn up with résumés that cost them anywhere from $100 to $300. Usually the résumés have been rendered in academic formats that are word-heavy and, frankly, just wrong for our industry. Candidates feel awful — and ripped off — when we tell them to redo them. We tell our candidates just to use ours. That's right, steal our formats. If you're uncomfortable with computers and prefer to use a résumé service, hand them our formats to use. We've been in business a long time now and, through lots of trial and error, we know what works.

A final point regarding your résumé: everything, absolutely everything in it must be accurate. Don't even think about fudging the dates or any numbers to inflate your record. If you do, it will come back to haunt you when, after you receive an offer, your prospective employer conducts a thorough background check based on the information you provide. Secondly, check, double-check, triple-check and then check everything you've written once again for errors. Give your résumé to at least four or five of your most capable and literate friends to proofread for typos and grammatical errors.

I can't begin to tell you how many typos we find in résumés. Managers, too, call us to complain when they find them. Typos make a bad first impression. Because they are so easily avoided, they are the worst way to undermine your prospects. They indicate a lack of attention to detail and general carelessness. Errors foreclose on the possibility of success, even before the real work of the job hunt has begun. There's no other way to say it: your résumé must be perfect — and it can be because you've got the time to hone it.

A great résumé can make the difference between whether you get in the door — or you don't.

## The Brag Book

What is a brag book? A brag book is a requirement for every prospective pharmaceutical sales representative. Traditionally, it consists of a professional-looking, 3-ring binder containing from 15 to 20 pages, many in plastic sleeves. Those plastic sleeves contain diplomas, letters of recommendation, awards, proof of sales rankings and other materials. Often candidates insert pages with subject tabs so that you and your interviewers can turn quickly to your sales documents or awards or other sections. The brag book supports and documents the information presented in your résumé and buttresses your case. It is an important tool you will use in telling your story to an interviewer, not simply a calling card to be left behind at the end of each meeting. One district manager I know says that during an interview a candidate should present his or her brag book to her interviewer as if he or she were already on the job using promotional materials to sell a new medication to a doctor. I recommend a cover page at the front in the following format. In this way, each brag book is personalized for each of your interviewers:

"Professional Presentation on Jane Doe

Prepared For Mr. John Smith with XYZ Pharmaceuticals"

Your Name

Street

City, State Zip

Phone

Email

- For added effect, you can put a good motivational quote on the top or bottom of your brag book cover.

The brag book is, then, made up of the following contents:

1) Your personal mission statement (optional, but recommended).
2) A copy of your résumé.
3) A copy of your college diploma.
4) A copy of your college transcripts (unless your grades aren't up to par).
5) Copies of stack rankings or anything that documents your actual sales numbers and sales accomplishments.
6) Performance reviews or evaluations (if they are positive).
7) Photocopies of plaques or awards you have won during your career.
8) Pictures of trophies you have won during the course of your career.
9) Copies of letters or emails from a manager that reward specific accomplishments.
10) Announcements from company newsletters regarding you, your performance or promotions.
11) Two to three letters from customers or letters of recommendation (but this is not as important as your actual numbers and results).
12) Three professional references, including their titles, your relationship to these individuals and their contact information including phone number and email.*

I recommend that my clients write a personal mission statement for the front of their brag book. In a short few lines, this tells your interviewer who you are as a person. Here is one sample:

# Personal Mission Statement for Jane Doe

1) I am goal-oriented. I set high, yet attainable goals. I am constantly reevaluating and setting new goals that motivate me.

2) I am committed to constantly learning and expanding my intellectual knowledge. This is done through reading, audio tapes, higher education, role modeling and constantly thirsting for new information on how to become a better human being.

3) I conduct my daily affairs with the "Golden Rule" at the forefront of my thinking in every interaction.

4) I exercise regularly to maintain my health and energy levels, as well as to keep stress at bay and maintain inner peace. I make sure to get enough sleep every night.

5) I am open to coaching and feedback to help me improve personally and professionally.

6) I am committed to being the best at everything I do.

The following are sample pages from a brag book. Many of our clients use print-outs of PowerPoint slides for their brag book pages.

---

*You need to make sure that you contact every person you list to ensure they will truly stand behind you and 'brag' about you if contacted. Don't leave this to chance, or you may regret it!

## Current Year
## Revenue Sales Stack Ranking 2006
## March 2006 YTD

| Marketing Rep | % | Account Manager | % | Specialists | % |
|---|---|---|---|---|---|
| Carol Adam | 130.2 | Hank Morris | 135.4 | Bob Law | 148.2 |
| Jim Pauls | 120.8 | JANE DOE | 134.9 | Lara Jones | 140.1 |
| Sam White | 115.5 | Ron Manor | 128.2 | Peter Wilson | 129.9 |
| Nick Robert | 110.5 | Rufus Greene | 117.0 | Kevin Song | 127.6 |
| Jack Saul | 108.2 | Vince Natte | 109.8 | Randy Beets | 103.2 |
| Ed Yamato | 103.7 | Luis Pena | 105.6 | Carl Kranhold | 101.8 |
| Andrew Ko | 100.3 | Mel Long | 104.9 | Sandy Updike | 99.0 |

# CLIMB TO REACH THE TOP

*Jane Doe*
X Corporation
Account Manager

----Original Message----
**From**: Smith, John
**Sent**: Tuesday, January 4, 2007
**To**: All Sales
**Subject**: Congratulations to Jane Doe!

It's official…. Jane Doe has qualified for the President's Club!

Also, congratulations to Jane for being the Top Marketing Rep in the nation! Jane, you are going to be STAR…. That is, a Star Award Winner!

Congratulations!

John Smith
Account Sales Manager
X Corporation

*Jane Doe*
X Corporation
Account Manager


---Original Message---
**From**: Kathy Jones
**Sent**: Tuesday, December 24, 2006
**To**: Management Team
**Subject**: Jane Doe

Dear Management,

FIND A WAY TO KEEP YOUR BEST REP HERE IN
CHICAGO!!!

We absolutely adore her. I just heard from Jane that she will be
relocating back to Los Angeles, and we are so sad to see her
go. But, if she must, I want to commend her for her hard work,
dedication and service to our account through the years. She is an
exceptional young lady who will be missed!

Jane's professionalism and her "go the extra mile" attitude is the
reason why we stayed with X Corporation.

We will miss her as I am sure you will as well!

Kind regards,

Kathy

Director of IT
JAX Technologies

*Jane Doe*
X Corporation
Account Manager


----Original Message----
**From:** Pam Green
**Sent:** Friday, December 1, 2006
**To:** John Smith, Jane Doe
**Subject**: My Sales Rep

Dear John,

I want to take a moment to write and let you know what an outstanding, amazing rep we have on our account. As you know, we have historically had difficulties with X Corporation representatives handling our account with a high turnover rate. Jane not only has stepped in, but has become the best rep we have ever had. We here at LMN have to commend her for her patience, her knowledge and her care towards her customers. You have a star here and we are so happy to have her on our team!

Please make sure the rest of the management staff receives this letter of appreciation, and I will see you next week at the demo!

Best,


Pam Green
VP of Operations
LMN Company

*Jane Doe*
X Corporation
Account Manager

----Original Message----
From: Brown, Linda
Sent: Friday, January 26, 2007
To: Doe, Jane
Subject: FW: Promotion-Jane Doe

Jane-

Congratulations on your well-deserved promotion. I am sure you will do a great job in the assignment. Let me know if I can be of any help to you.

Linda

----Original Message----
From: Thompson, John
Sent: Friday, January 26, 2007
To: All Sales
Subject: Promotion-Jane Doe

It's with a great deal of pleasure that I announce the promotion of Jane Doe to Account Manager effective February 1. Jane will be taking over the XR04 assignment reporting to me.

Jane has done an excellent job in her Marketing Representative assignment earning not one, but two Star Awards as the top Marketing Representative in X Corporation. In addition, Jane is off to a fast start in 2007, on her way to achieving K Club for her 1st quarter performance.

Please join me in congratulating Jane on her promotion.

Sincerely,

John Thompson
GM, Managed Services
X Corporation

# Some people dream of success ... while others wake up and work hard at it.

Author Unknown

# Top 10 Reasons Why You Should Hire Jane

- Goal-driven
- Organized
- Creative
- Solution-oriented
- Ambitious
- Motivated and Energetic
- Aggressive and Tenacious
- Ethical
- Problem Solver
- Self-starting

*Sad But True:* Once we had a candidate who made the mistake of listing as a reference someone he hardly knew to impress his interviewer with the individual's position in a Fortune 500 company. You can guess what happened. The interviewer called, and the reference did not know the job candidate. Ask for trouble, and you're likely to get it.

If you really want to make a meaningful impression, include a reference who may not have a fancy title, but who really knows you and who can speak with great specificity to your strengths and experience. You want that individual who will attest to your work ethic and sing your praises until he or she is blue in the face. Make sure every person you include is among your biggest fans and supporters.

Lastly, I recommend making several color copies of your brag book. The majority of interviewers will ask you to leave the book for later review. It is far better to come prepared, with extra copies, than to have to apologize for having only one to leave behind. This telegraphs a failure to adequately prepare. Your interviewers will immediately imagine this happening in a doctor's office, with forgotten business cards or product samples. The result: a missed opportunity, the failure to close a deal.

If you are already asking yourself whether or not you want to go to so much trouble to find a job in this industry, then I'd suggest you set this book aside and consider a career in another field.

If, however, you are still excited for the challenges ahead, then read on. You are the person I want to be talking to.

# CHAPTER FOUR

# Research

*❝ Know your enemy, know yourself, and your victory will not be threatened. Know the terrain, know the weather, and your victory will be complete. ❞*

**— Sun Tzu, The Art of War, 500 B.C.**

Many candidates make the mistake of thinking the interview alone is the most important part of finding a job in pharmaceutical sales. It is not. Preparing for the interview is the most critical part of your search. In the next two chapters, I'll show you how to network and get the interviews themselves — but you need to do some preparatory research before you approach anyone. People either succeed or fail based on the amount of research and preparation they've done prior to the interview. Inadequate preparation and research can immediately handicap your chances before you even think of walking into an interview. The deciding factors — especially in this market when the competition is so stiff — will be these:

- **Who has done the most thorough research?**
- **Which candidate does the best job of marshaling that research effectively during the interview and hiring process?**

In our survey of district managers, most emphasized the crucial role of research. One of them put it this way: "I have interviewed people who did not know anything beyond the name of the company and products they were potentially going to sell. If I see that they have not researched the company's products (and don't have) at least a top-line understanding of the disease states, they are out of the running for me. Experienced in the industry or not — they are out."

A district manager and friend from a Fortune 500 pharmaceutical company always asks candidates he interviews to tell him in great detail exactly how they prepared for the interview. He strongly recommends that you role-play your answers to questions such as these. Before he broke into the industry himself, he sat with his wife on the family couch for hours while she played interviewer, quizzing him so that he could role-play all his responses. Another experienced executive I know in the industry recorded his voice and then played it back — something he learned in a speech class. He was surprised to discover how quickly he spoke. Listen to your voice and work on your pacing. Notice how well you articulate your thoughts. Is your inflection pitch-perfect — or a little off? Do you insert too many — or too few — pauses?

Think back to college and your experience taking final exams. How did you feel walking into a final exam knowing that you did not prepare as thoroughly as you should have? You open the classroom door, and you meekly walk into a room filled with your peers. You are conscious of the fact that — unlike you — they have been studying and preparing for this moment. You think back over the previous two weeks of the school year. You realize you did a little too much socializing, went to a few too many parties and drank a few too many beers when you should have been holed up at the library hitting the books. That sinking feeling hits you in the stomach, and a wave of panic sets in. How did you feel when you walked into the room? Unless you were one of those students who didn't need to study (unlike me), your self-confidence was probably not very high.

Conversely, how did you feel when you hit the books hard, studied and prepared for weeks and months prior to the final exams, met with fellow students to role-play possible questions and answers and met regularly with the professor or teacher's assistant to make sure you knew what to expect come test time? Chances are your confidence soared as you walked into those final exams.

If you follow my plan, you'll walk into each of your interviews feeling confident, knowing you are primed and ready. Here are the main courses of action I recommend, with more detail on each to come:

1. Start with the Internet. Research the companies with which you plan to interview, their competitors and their drug offerings.
2. If at all possible at this stage, go for a ride-along (also known as a field ride or a field preceptorship) with a pharmaceutical sales representative.

3. Call the Customer Service department at the company with which your interview is scheduled and ask to speak with someone who can answer general questions about the company.

4. Ask your doctor and pharmacist about their experiences with the company with which your interview is scheduled.

5. Talk to representatives themselves — one of the best strategies. The next chapter is largely devoted to teaching you how to do this.

# 1. The Internet

The Internet is a remarkable tool to help you break into pharmaceutical sales. In our survey of more than 150 sales representatives, 50% said the Internet was the best resource they found for researching the industry. Before you contact anybody, spend some time delving into the websites of the major pharmaceutical companies — especially those that interest you. In the Investor Relations sections, take a look at the opening statements by the company leadership. The chairman's letter to the shareholders or the introduction by the company president usually gives an overview of the last year as well as a forecast of the company's direction for the next year. This is a great summary, usually two to four pages long. After this letter, there will be a section discussing the future. This is a very important section. You will learn about how the company is handling current challenges in the marketplace. It will also address new drugs in the pipeline, as well as the amount of money allocated for research and development (R&D). Make sure to review the financial highlights, especially overall revenues, revenue growth projections and the R&D budget.

Try to get a sense of the "feel" of the company by reading between the lines a bit. Some companies cultivate an approachable, people-oriented culture; others emphasize numbers and science. You can't always get a true picture of the company culture from a website, but you might turn up some telling clues which would indicate whether this is going to be a good fit for you.

The following websites provide valuable industry-wide information.

www.cafehealthcare.com
www.cafepharma.com (sign up for their daily pharma headlines)
www.finance.yahoo.com (sign up for email alerts on companies)

www.forbes.com/business (sign up for email alerts on companies)
www.fortune.com
www.google.com/alerts (sign up for email alerts on companies)
www.healthtouch.com
www.hirerx.com
www.jobsaledirectory.com
www.hoovers.com
www.indeed.com
www.mypharmaceuticaljob.com
www.money.cnn.com
www.napsronline.org
www.Pdrhealth.com
www.pharmaceuticaljob.com
www.pharmaceuticaljobs-usa.com
www.pharmaopportunities.com
www.pharmrep.com
www.phrma.org
www.tomruff.com
www.topix.net/business/pharmaceuticals/pr
www.webmd.com
www.wetfeet.com

# 2. The ride-along

We examine ride-alongs in even greater detail in later chapters because they can be a make-or-break part of the interview process. However, the most proactive job candidates spend a day riding along with working pharmaceutical representatives even before securing interviews. Spend two or three days if you can. A good ride-along may get you that crucial first interview. This is most easily done, of course, if you know people in the industry. However, if you do not, use some of the tips I gave for meeting them in Chapter Two. And, as I mentioned before, make sure to introduce yourself by saying right up front that you are on a job hunt. Representatives do sometimes find themselves answering detailed questions from FDA investigators and may be suspicious if you don't let them know what you're after right away. If you do get a chance to ride along with a pharmaceutical representative, it will give you the most tangible, real-world sense of what the job entails. You'll get to see a representative navigating the sometimes tricky world of hospitals and busy doctors' offices, vying for face time with professionals who are working under constant pressure to serve patients and demanding health care systems.

> *"It's always impressive if someone took the time to do a field preceptorship (ride-along)."*
> — **Jennifer Abram, former sales recruiter with Johnson & Johnson**

If you manage to ride along with a sales representative this early in the game, you can use the impressions you've gathered throughout the rest of your interview process. You will put it on your résumé under the heading "Field Preceptorship." This is industry jargon which means you've spent time in the field with an expert. This will jump out on your résumé and get your foot in the door. Although it's highly advisable to do one, surprisingly, the vast majority of job seekers do not.

## 3. Call the Customer Service department

Once you've got an interview scheduled — but *before* you have it — call the Customer Service department of the pharmaceutical company with which you will be interviewing. Tell them that you have an interview scheduled with their company, and ask if someone might be willing to spend a few minutes on the phone answering a couple of your questions.

When you call, be unfailingly polite. This strategy is most effective at the smaller pharmaceutical companies which, according to Hay Group, represent the fastest-growing segment in the industry. With fewer levels of bureaucracy, the person you speak with may call the district manager you plan to meet to tell him or her about you. This has happened to a couple of our clients. It's yet another way to make a strong impression, to differentiate yourself from the field and to better prepare for the interview.

Sometimes you may be given a sales representative's contact information or be transferred to someone else. Make sure you are prepared with your list of questions. If someone does take your call, don't waste their time. Get as much information as possible — all of it will help in the interview — and take good notes.

Here are some good questions to ask:

1) How would you describe your corporate culture?
2) What does it take to be successful at your company?
3) Do you know this district manager?
4) If so, can you tell me anything about his/her interviewing style?
5) Can you think of any tips that might help me to do well in the interview?
6) What do you like about working for this company?
7) What are some challenges you've experienced that I should be aware of?
8) Are you familiar with the following drugs? (Ask specifically about the drugs you would be selling and what attributes are most important to mention.)

At the end of the conversation, make sure you take down the person's name and contact information. As with almost everyone you meet as you break into this new career, you will want to send him or her a handwritten thank-you note. Your thoughtfulness may prompt another call, upon receipt of that letter, to the all-important district manager. The more people you've got pulling for you in an organization, the better.

One thing you will want to try to ascertain through your research is just what kind of companies are out there. The personalities and needs of each pharmaceutical company vary widely.

Not long ago, we sent a bright and energetic candidate to interview with a large pharmaceutical company. The district manager passed on him, bluntly dismissing him in an email, from which we partially quote, "Communication and impact not there.... Blanked on a few things." We were surprised. While expressing our regret, we were also glad to be able to tell our client that the individual in question had just received an offer from a competitor, who couldn't have been more excited to make the hire. A candidate who would not be hired by one company may be a perfect fit at another.

Over the years, we've made some observations about the general preferences in each of the large companies. In our considered and admittedly very subjective opinion, here are a few examples:

## Characteristics of Top Companies

Abbott — Values candidates with the strongest interpersonal skills and most aggressive sales abilities.

Forest — Looks for candidates with an aggressive, proven approach to business-to-business sales.

GlaxoSmithKline — Favors conservative personalities with proven track records and the ability to pass tough pharmacological entrance tests.

Johnson & Johnson — Prefers polished candidates with strong, documented sales experience and impressive GPAs.

Merck — Puts great stock in clinical know-how and/or experience.

Pfizer — Looks for people with leadership experience and values a military record.

## 4. Talk with your own doctor and dentist, their office managers and your pharmacist

Your physicians have a vested interest in maintaining an ongoing relationship with you, as one of their clients. We've found that our candidates have good luck asking their health care providers about their experiences with their preferred pharmaceutical companies and representatives. In fact, they'll give you the lowdown, without sugar coating. In all likelihood, they've had experience with representatives whom they disliked or found bothersome, as well as others with whom they may have developed strong professional friendships. Find out what they liked or disliked in both instances.

A physician I know in South Bend, Indiana, Dr. David Clayton (read more from him in Chapter 18) has good things to say about the six to ten representatives who visit his office daily: "They are an excellent resource because they tell me about new drugs before I may read about them. They give me scientific articles to review as to how this particular medication may fit into my treatment plan. They are kind enough to pass along samples that we can then share with our patients, particularly those who don't have drug prescription coverage or maybe they are just really tight financially." David has, at times, passed on the résumés of job candidates to pharmaceutical companies. A couple of them have gotten jobs.

Ask the doctors you visit for their perceptions of each of the pharmaceutical companies and, if their time permits, the different drugs they most commonly prescribe. If you can, get specific information about drug side effects and interactions, and about competing drugs from other companies.

Make sure you also talk with the office manager or office staff. Their opinions influence the doctors' views of the different pharmaceutical sales representatives calling on them. Their perceptions will be telling and valuable. They may have more time to talk about your quest than a doctor, surgeon or dentist will. These conversations will greatly round out your research into the industry and demonstrate that you are already getting to know a very important group of people — your future customers.

IMPORTANT NOTE: While you are in doctors' offices, make sure to request contact information for any and all of the pharmaceutical representatives who call on them regularly. If possible, ask a receptionist or office manager to copy all of their business cards. If not, you might also see if you could run them over to a local copy shop and copy them yourself. The office staff often has stacks of these cards.

Ask the doctor or office manager if you could use his or her name as a reference when you contact the sales representatives. In the following chapter I'll tell you what to do next.

## TOM'S TIP — HANDWRITTEN NOTES

AS I'VE MENTIONED ELSEWHERE, make sure to send handwritten thank-you notes to each and every one of the people you met with at this stage. Look at it this way: when you open your mail every day, which letters do you open first? If you're like me, you start with anything that someone took the time to write by hand.

WITH THE DAWN OF ELECTRONIC COMMUNICATIONS, many people thought that handwritten communications would simply disappear. In many ways, they have. But, at the same time, handwritten letters have taken on a greater currency.

PEOPLE APPRECIATE THE TIME YOU TAKE to put your thoughts down in ink on paper, to affix a stamp to an envelope and to drop that note in the mail.

I TAKE THE TIME TO WRITE OUT HANDWRITTEN THANK-YOUS and notes of appreciation regularly. Often I accompany them with newspaper or magazine articles about subjects of interest to my friends or business associates. Sometimes I send books along with my notes. They are a tangible demonstration of the value I place on my relationships — in business and in my personal life.

# CHAPTER FIVE

# Networking

**❝** If you want to catch beasts you don't see every day,
You have to go places quite out-of-the-way.
You have to go places no others can get to.
You have to get cold and you have to get wet, too. **❞**

**— Dr. Seuss**

The old adage, "It's not *what* you know, but *who* you know" is nowhere more relevant than in the pharmaceutical sales job search. Networking is a must for anyone looking to break in. Preliminary networking is part of the research phase of your hunt, which we've just discussed. But in order to get those key interviews, you've got to muster a little more creativity and fearlessness. People you hardly know or haven't yet met may help you the most. Here's a quote from best-selling author Malcolm Gladwell's *The Tipping Point* that explains why this is so:

> ...(W)hen it comes to finding out about new jobs... "weak ties" are always more important than strong ties. Your friends, after all, occupy the same world that you do. They might work with you, or live near you, and go to the same churches, schools or parties. How much, then, would they know that you wouldn't know? Your acquaintances, on the other hand, by definition occupy a very different world than you. They are much more likely to know something that you don't. To capture this apparent paradox, (sociologist Mark) Granovetter coined a marvelous phrase: "the strength of weak ties." Acquaintances, in short, represent a source of social power, and the more acquaintances you have, the more powerful you are.

Here are my top networking sources for building new and powerful "weak ties," followed by greater detail on each.

# Tom Ruff's Top Networking Sources

1) Doctors' and Dentists' Offices
2) Pharmacists
3) Family
4) Friends
5) Colleagues and former co-workers
6) Grass-roots email campaign
7) Reputable pharmaceutical recruiting firms
8) Pharmaceutical networking meetings
9) Hospitals
10) Internet (includes helpful websites)
11) Tradeshows
12) Job fairs
13) Trade magazines
14) Newspaper classified advertisements
15) Books and directories

## NETWORKING — Doctors' and Dentists' Offices

### The doctor's office, medical centers, dentists and surgeons

One of the best ways to break into the pharmaceutical sales industry is to have a working sales representative recommend you for a position within his or her company. "But I don't know any pharmaceutical sales representatives," you say. Soon you will. Meeting them is easier than you think.

If you've followed my tips in the last chapter, then you've already collected cards from a handful of pharmaceutical sales representatives from your doctor's or dentist's office, or from your surgeon or pharmacist.

Now it's time to put them to work.

With any luck, you've secured permission to use the name of your own doctor and dentist or their officer managers as references. Once a sales representative sees you've been referred by a key doctor or office manager, you are almost guaranteed a reply. Their relationship with that doctor is too important to jeopardize in any way. They don't have to know *how* you got their contact information. The mere fact that you did will be enough. Furthermore, most companies offer their sales representatives commissions of between $1,000 and $3,000 for each new hire they bring in. They will be predisposed to give you a fair hearing.

One additional and important point is that, if you do have a strong relationship with specific doctors, you can also use them as references in your brag book. They will make a persuasive case for you in the application process. So work at cultivating those contacts.

The best way to contact pharmaceutical representatives is by email. If you have permission to use a referral, put the doctor's name in the subject line of the message. That's sure to get a response. In my survey of both district managers and representatives, several respondents made the point that a colorful or highly specific subject line will ensure the email is read. One wrote: "In my opinion, the subject line should be the candidate's theme or tagline, the common thread that connects everything throughout the entire process...the X factor. The X factor means, 'Does this person have something that will lead me to open, explore and forward (with a personal recommendation) yet another résumé?' To sell this person, I'd want to be pretty confident that they will not only elevate the level of our team but also that they will make me look good in the interview." So, don't forget the subject line!

Most representatives said they do respond to emails, so send away. As with your résumé, be very brief and to the point.

## *Sample Email to Pharmaceutical Sales Representatives*

I was referred to you by Dr. John Doe in Austin. I am very interested in breaking into pharmaceutical sales with Your Company and he suggested you could help. I have three years of successful outside sales experience. My sole focus now is to break into pharmaceutical sales. I have talked at length to my doctor, researched the industry thoroughly and spoken with several other pharmaceutical sales representatives, one of whom I accompanied on a ride-along.

I am confident in my ability to secure a position within your firm. Would you be willing to forward my email and résumé to your District Manager or advise me of the best approach to secure an interview with your company? I would not waste you or your manager's time.

Thank you for your consideration, and for any assistance you might be able to provide.

Sincerely,
Jane Doe
Phone
Email address

Pharmaceutical representatives are very busy. Always be polite and never be pushy. Working representatives field a constant stream of requests from job seekers. One of my friends tells me that he is constantly frustrated and amazed by the rude and inconsiderate behavior of the job-seekers who contact him. One woman called him six times over a two-day stretch. The final call rang in at 11 p.m. while my friend was up doing paperwork. When my friend answered the phone, the woman berated him for not returning her call, making no apology for the late hour.

With such behavior, there was nothing my friend could or would do to help her. How would she treat a doctor or a pharmacist?

Another word of caution about approaching a pharmaceutical representative: if you've gotten wind that one may be replaced by his or her company, do not contact this individual. Even if you only suspect this may be the case, refrain from making the call. Twice in the past we've had a candidate who, while making networking calls, inadvertently alerted a representative that he or she was about to lose his job. After talking to our candidate, one working representative picked up the phone and asked his district manager, "Are you interviewing for my position?" Needless to say, it was uncomfortable for all involved.

Again, remember to be exceptionally attentive to the pressures to perform that working pharmaceutical sales representatives face daily. When you do reach one on the phone, always start the conversation by asking,

"Is this a good time to talk?" If not, try to settle on a more convenient time, but never call back more than a couple of times a week. You risk making a bad impression. You'll be better served by finding a different and more receptive person through one of the many channels we discuss in this chapter.

If a sales representative does indeed help you to secure an interview, stay in touch. Keep him or her informed of your interview status, with regular updates via emails or phone calls (depending on this individual's preferences) at every step along the way.

If you need advice as you go through subsequent interviews — and if you've developed a good relationship with this representative — contact him or her for input on the person who will conduct your next interview.

Finally, as always, send a handwritten thank-you note to any sales representative who helps you along the way. As I've mentioned before, it's a simple gesture, but a powerful one. It speaks to your thoughtfulness, diligence and attention to detail. It will bring your name repeatedly in front of people who may find themselves in a position to advocate for you.

One of our candidates sent flowers to the sales representative who helped her land her very first interview. The two forged a wonderful friendship, and the candidate credited her job offer in large part to the steady stream of careful and thorough guidance she received.

As I've said, the working drug representative can be your best advocate. Ideally, you will be joining them in their profession. Use the Golden Rule. Treat them with all the care and solicitude that you would hope to receive were you in their shoes. The respect you show will pay substantial dividends down the road.

## NETWORKING — Pharmacists

When you visit your local pharmacy, use the same approach you used with your doctor and dentist. Pharmacies are even busier places than doctors' offices, so it's important to visit during non-peak hours when you'll have a chance for a meaningful discussion with the pharmacist on duty.

Again, you must be respectful of the pharmacist's time. In your job hunt, you are practicing the very same skills you will need to perfect in order to succeed as a pharmaceutical sales representative. So, don't take the job hunt component lightly.

Explain your quest to the pharmacist. As with the doctor's office, ask for business cards from any pharmaceutical sales representatives that you can copy by hand or with a machine. Most drug stores have a copier behind the counter. If you make this request off-hours, the people there will be much more likely to make these copies for you. Ask the pharmacist for permission to use his or her name as a referral.

Once you email a pharmaceutical sales representative, wait for about a week before sending a follow-up. You should be contacting so many that you won't be troubled by a slow response from some of them. Concentrate on volume. Focus your energy where you are getting a return. Follow up most quickly with those who follow up with you. Keep in mind that these individuals must plow through hundreds and hundreds of emails every week so wait for an appropriate period of time if you don't hear anything. Yours may very well have become lost in the deluge.

Later in the process, when you have an interview scheduled and know what medications you need to research for the interview, you will want to research these drugs.

**The following is a list of questions about medications you can ask of both pharmacists and doctors to elicit the most useful information:**

- What is your opinion of this medication?
- Which type of patient would you prescribe this product for? Why?
- Which are the competing products?
- What advantages and disadvantages does this medication have compared to other drugs in its class?
- What is the safety profile of this drug compared to other drugs in its class?
- What are the side effects? Are there any side effects you pay particular attention to?
- Does this drug have any significant interactions?
- How is it metabolized (i.e., in the liver, elsewhere in the body)?
- What is this drug's managed care status? Is it covered by most managed care companies? Is it covered by Medicaid?

- Do you prescribe this medication in conjunction with other drugs?
- Is it taken once a day or b.i.d. (Latin for "twice a day")?

Later, once you've secured interviews, it is essential to learn which of these companies' medications are generally covered by patients' insurance. It is a tremendous advantage for a pharmaceutical company to have its products covered by insurance. Those drugs are easier for doctors to prescribe and more affordable for patients. If you work for a company whose drugs are not covered, your job will be much more difficult.

## NETWORKING — Family

So you haven't spoken with Uncle George or your second cousin's wife's brother-in-law lately? Not even this decade? Well, now is the time to renew the acquaintance. Seriously, an earnest job hunt can be a wonderful starting point to renew a connection that dropped off long ago. As with the doctor, pharmacist and dental office, make sure to show great care and respect to your own family. You may come to see them in a new light and learn a thing or two about your history.

In the meantime — and this, of course, is the ultimate point — you may find that one of them knows a pharmaceutical sales representative or someone else in the industry who could be of help to you.

If your relatives don't know anyone in the industry, ask if they have a good relationship with their physicians and/or dentists and possibly with their office managers. With these phone numbers and addresses in hand, you have a whole new selection of leads with a new group of pharmaceutical sales representatives.

See what you can discover out along the branches of your family tree.

## NETWORKING — Friends

For all those times you let your buddy borrow your favorite golf clubs or you babysat for your college roommate who lives 45 minutes away, guess what? It's time to call in a few chits of your own.

Find out who they know who works in the industry. It could be a member of their family, someone at their place of worship or a neighbor — one of their own "weak ties." When they search their minds, you'll want details, full names spelled as correctly as possible and digits — phone numbers and email addresses. The industry is growing so rapidly that, chances are, somebody among your broad acquaintance will know somebody who knows somebody who knows somebody. You may be starting to feel like a private eye at this point, which is not a bad thing. Even if some people don't come up with a name, ask them to ask their own friends and family this question for you. In all likelihood, you will uncover still more contacts. Put all of them into a database on your computer, using a program like Excel, to keep track of everyone you will eventually contact and to monitor the number, frequency, substance and helpfulness of your communications.

This is a real numbers game. All the energy that you put out into the universe will come back to you.

## NETWORKING — Colleagues and Former Co-Workers

If you are still employed, use caution as you consider who to confide in about your job hunt. Make sure you speak only with people you trust enough to know they will not tell others about your plans. One good source of contacts is to look into the paths taken by those who have left your company to go elsewhere. Especially if you are working in sales right now, or in a healthcare-related field, one or more of your former colleagues may have taken a job somewhere in the pharmaceutical industry. If so, and if you can trust them, get in contact and see what you can learn from them. This contact can be both part of your research and your networking process. They may have helpful tips or suggestions.

If one of them has recently landed a job, they will have excellent interviewing advice. In all probability, they have interviewed with many potential employers on the way to finding a job. Having just gone through the ringer, they will probably be eager to share their war stories and their highly subjective views of the process. Soak it all up. Take down the names of individuals they encountered and their suggestions about how to approach them. Their insights will be invaluable — potentially even more so than a working pharmaceutical sales representative who has been with one company for a number of years and is somewhat removed from the current job market, which is in constant flux.

Of course, ask if their own company is hiring, and if they could recommend you to someone to secure an interview of your own.

# NETWORKING — Grass-roots Email Campaign

Email has become an incredible networking tool, if used properly. To simplify your hunt, craft a compelling email and send it — quite literally — to everyone you know: friends, family members and business contacts. Include your new network of contacts in the pharmaceutical industry, so that these individuals can glimpse your personal marketing efforts at work.

I recommend against sending a mass email anonymously. Even if you are sending out a list to a hundred of your friends, you will get a better response if you take the time to personalize each one with an individual's name up top. Sure it takes more time, but isn't your future worth it?

You will be amazed at how many new contacts you will drum up over email alone. Howard Dean went from being a virtual unknown to a national political figure thanks to the Internet in the run-up to the 2004 presidential election. But the lesson of Dean's campaign is that the Web is not for micromanagers. According to information technology publication *Baseline* magazine, "With the Internet, an effective campaign creates a community that will on its own begin to market your product for you. Properly done, you won't be able — or want — to control it." Here's how to start your own viral campaign.

## *Sample email to your network*

I am writing this confidential email to request your assistance and support in finding a position in pharmaceutical sales. I have three years of successful business-to-business outside sales experience including two President's Club Awards, a #1 sales ranking in my region out of 55 of my colleagues and I'm currently tracking at 145% of quota, year-to-date. I am looking to parlay this successful track record into a position within the growing field of pharmaceutical sales.

## *If you know of ...*

– Any pharmaceutical sales representatives

– Anyone who works for a pharmaceutical company

– Any pharmaceutical companies that are hiring right now

... please let me know, or feel free to forward this email, along with my résumé, to these individuals.


In addition:

If you have a good relationship with your doctor or the office manager in your doctor's office, please let me know. I would like to contact them directly to request the names and contact information for the sales representatives that call on them.

I can be reached via email:_____or phone: _____

I greatly appreciate your support. And if I can do anything for you in return, please let me know.

Sincerely,
Your Name
Your email
Your phone number


Now you can let your network go to work for you. That's a lot of power at your fingertips.

# NETWORKING — Reputable Pharmaceutical Recruiting Firms

No one knows the exact number but, nationwide, there are hundreds of firms right now that specialize in recruiting for pharmaceutical sales positions. Many of them offer high-quality services. Many of them do not. You will need to ask around in the industry as you contact people to see which ones can offer you the best service and the best chance of breaking into a top pharmaceutical company.

**A cautionary note:** if you choose to go this route, do not — I repeat, do not — submit your résumé to companies through their websites without *first* checking with the recruiter you are working with. Applying online will immediately disqualify you as a candidate for a recruiter working with those companies. Recruiters stake their reputations on offering to their client companies only talent that can be found nowhere else. A pharmaceutical company won't pay a recruiter to find you if that company already has a copy of your résumé in its system. About once a week, we lose the chance to represent viable candidates because they've already begun their own search online. It's a source of constant frustration.

Some recruiters have access to job openings within top companies that are available nowhere else because of exclusive contracts they have signed to fill the positions for the clients. There are a number of pharmaceutical companies that rely on these exclusive relationships because they find them to be the most effective means of reaching top-quality candidates. In fact, in the proprietary survey I conducted with district managers, nearly half said they hired most of their representatives through recruiters (see Chapter 15 for the full survey results.) With interest in these positions so strong, companies' internal hiring departments sometimes find the work of plowing through résumés from the general population an inefficient use of their time and resources. That said, many of the larger companies are getting better at hunting in order to reduce their hiring costs.

If you have outside sales experience and a strong track record of success, working with a reputable recruiter can be a fast and efficient way of breaking in.

As I mentioned earlier, the operative word in the last sentence is "reputable." As in any industry there is a select group of ethical, effective recruiters out there, and there is another group that does not adhere to ethical business standards. You need to be as selective in choosing a recruiter as you are in choosing an employer. One common, wrong-headed tactic of unscrupulous recruiters is to send your résumé to hundreds of people in different companies with total disregard for the confidentiality of your job search. Given the speed with which information travels over the Internet, you never know whose inbox your résumé may land in. It could be your current employer's. It has happened.

My suggestion to you is to find the best recruiter specializing in pharmaceutical sales in your local marketplace. Several high-quality firms operate nationally, but we've found that a local focus helps a recruiter to understand the dynamics of the marketplace in your geographical area.

Here are some approaches I recommend for finding a good pharmaceutical recruiting firm.

## *How to find the best recruiting firms:*

1) Go to the US-Recruiters national website directory at www.us-recruiters.com/region.html.

2) Ask all of your friends, colleagues and family members if they have heard good things about any firms in particular.

3) Ask this same question of all the pharmaceutical sales representatives you come in contact with. Find out if they themselves used recruiters and ask them to tell you about their experiences.

4) Do a Google search for "pharmaceutical sales recruiter" and the city or state that you are looking in. Once you get a couple of names, conduct further research into each one. Mention those names to each of the people you encounter in the industry.

5) Lastly, dig out the good, old-fashioned Yellow Pages. Look under "Employment Agencies" for recruiters specializing in this field. Then do more research on those names via the Internet and through the networking channels you are establishing.

Recruiting firms do offer a key strategic advantage — they can help you pierce through the noise of applying online. If you submit over the Web (more on this in a minute), you will be vying against hundreds — if not thousands — of résumés that are submitted directly to pharmaceutical companies. It is possible to secure an interview in this manner; companies often fill primary care sales positions with Web candidates. But it is also possible, when you're up against numbers like these, to be lost in the résumé black hole. The top pharmaceutical companies are still perfecting the process of separating the wheat from the chaff among the résumés they receive. They lose some great candidates as a result.

A friend of mine who worked as a sales recruiter for a major pharmaceutical company sometimes used to test her employer's Web filters to see what would happen. She would go online and fill out questionnaires candidates are required to complete and submit along with their résumés. "I'd use my own résumé," she says, "I have a lot of experience, but sometimes the way I answered one or two questions would knock me out."

Once, she answered yes when asked if she works well with others, a pretty universally positive skill. But, the website seemed to interpret the response to indicate that she would not be a self starter — an impression that she didn't intend to convey and that was, in any case, inaccurate.

"This is one of the flaws of these websites. The interpretation is so subjective," she says. However, companies are taking measures to fix this tendency and make the knock-out questions less sensitive.

A good recruiting firm — one with strong relationships with its client firms — can be the difference between finding a job or not. Working with a recruiter, you will generally find yourself facing a field of only eight to ten competitors vying for that same position. This, of course, will depend on the strengths you bring to the table. Ask a recruiter for some honest feedback as to whether or not they realistically think they can get you an interview, or if you should apply to companies on your own. A good one won't beat around the bush.

To give you a more detailed idea about how to work successfully with a recruiter once you find one, see Chapter 16.

## NETWORKING — Pharmaceutical Networking Groups

Among the hidden gems in the world of pharmaceutical sales representatives — one that most job seekers are completely unaware of — is the pharmaceutical representative association.

Members of these associations meet regularly, some monthly and others quarterly, throughout the year. Typically they discuss what works and what doesn't work in their industry. Company names and names of drugs are banned from these meetings in acknowledgement of the highly competitive world in which the members operate. It is a safe place for working representatives, where day-to-day market realities are discussed with candor.

If you could gain admittance to one of these meetings, you would accomplish several key goals at once. You would not only be able to research your new profession thoroughly, but you would come away with up-to-the-minute inside information.

Even more important, you would have access to a great number of pharmaceutical representatives in one place, and at a time when they are at greater leisure and not surrounded by other job hunters. Usually, the gatherings include a happy hour, which creates a relaxed, convivial setting for meeting people.

"We've never had anyone come visit that I can remember," says Robert Evans, a divisional trainer of Sanofi-Aventis, who's been a member of the Michiana Pharmaceutical Representative Association in South Bend, Indiana for four years. "But it would be an incredible way to find out about openings, learn about each company and get some great information."

At the end of each meeting, leaders usually ask if any of the companies represented are hiring, if there is anyone in attendance who is looking for a new job and if anyone knows of anybody who is looking for a job. What a golden opportunity! Stand up and introduce yourself to the group. If you're shy, pretend you are somebody who isn't. Pretend you are auditioning for a role in a play. In a very real sense, you are. You're auditioning for a role in your new career.

Evans recommends asking drug representatives for information about their local associations. In our appendix, on page 226, we have reproduced the list of drug representative associations from *Pharmaceutical Representative* magazine. You can check that same list online for updates at:

www.pharmrep.com/pharmrep/static/staticHtml.jsp?id=101197

When calling an association, request permission to attend in order to learn more about the industry. Once you are in the door, the rest is up to you. Make sure to bring a stack of résumés and brag books in a briefcase.

As always, collect as many business cards as you possibly can. Send follow-up emails that night. Networking is the name of the game.

## NETWORKING — Hospitals

Be bold. Be different. Be daring. We've already discussed the effectiveness of standing in front of hospitals, flagging down working pharmaceutical representatives and getting their business cards. Despite the fact that doing so is a surefire way to impress an interviewer, it always astonishes me how few people take advantage of this strategy, which is open to any and all. Join the 1% who do, and you will set yourself apart from the crowd.

## NETWORKING — Internet

Without even leaving your home, you can still score interviews, using the power of the Internet.

As I mentioned earlier, just know that if you submit your résumé directly to a company, you disqualify yourself from working with a recruiter, whose value to hiring companies is predicated on their exclusive line to you.

That said, many people do indeed secure interviews with pharmaceutical companies directly through those companies' websites. Visit tomruff. com to find a list of "The Top Pharmaceutical Companies to Work For." On page 191 you will also find a list. We provide links to each company's website as well as general contact information and other vital statistics.

Typically the job openings are posted in the Career or Jobs section of each site. Look for openings in your local area. Then do a search by date, listing the most recent postings first. Unfortunately, some companies are slow in updating these listings, some of which may have already been filled. While you are in your job hunt mode, check back with these listings on a daily basis. The key is to submit your résumé as soon as a new opening is posted.

One way to work with a recruiter and to submit your résumé directly to companies is to ascertain which companies your chosen recruiter works with. If your recruiter does not work with a company that interests you — and if he or she is ethical — you may be advised to go ahead and submit a résumé on your own.

Job boards such as Monster.com or Hotjobs.com can also be a great resource for finding pharmaceutical sales positions. In my experience, candidates do not make enough use of these sites. Hotjobs, part of Yahoo!, allows you to set up a My Yahoo! Page, which can be customized by uploading your résumé. When you find job openings, you will be able to submit your résumé directly without uploading it over and over again. Job openings that meet your criteria will be emailed to you when they become available. If you decide to make your résumé searchable, you will enable companies to find and contact you as they conduct Internet searches for job candidates. Many other job sites have competing features such as these. If you take the time to make use of these sites, and then put them to work for you, they can be tremendous tools.

www.careerbuilder.com
www.careersinpharmaceutical.com
www.Hotjobs.com
www.medzilla.com
www.Monster.com
www.pharmaceuticaljobs-usa.com
www.pharmaopportunities.com
www.tomruff.com

## NETWORKING — Tradeshows

Pharmaceutical tradeshows can be the mother lode for breaking into the pharmaceutical sales industry. Imagine being in a room of hundreds — maybe even a thousand — sales representatives and district managers from all the top pharmaceutical companies, not only in the United States but around the world. It takes a little creativity to gain admission to an industry trade show, but I'll show you how. You won't find more contacts assembled in the same spot anywhere.

Start with the website for your local convention center, and then try websites for other convention centers you'd be willing to drive — or fly — to. There you will find out which pharmaceutical or healthcare conventions are coming to town.

Next, you'll need to find a way to get in. Some of the tradeshows are open to the general public, for a fee, which can range anywhere from

$100 to $1,000. It might sound expensive, but it may be a real investment in your future. (Use the money you would have spent on a résumé-writing service).

If it is not open to the general public, email or call everyone in the pharmaceutical network you've been building to find out if they, or someone in their company, will be attending the show. If so, ask if you could contact the right person to see if you might obtain a guest pass or get some additional help from them to get you in.

Do what it takes, within reason, to get in. Direct contact and face time with hiring managers, whether they have an opening or not, is an extraordinarily effective means of making your case. The high price barrier may even work in your favor if — as has happened — you are the only job hunter working the entire convention. This will certainly set you apart. I've spoken with district managers who made hires largely on the impressions that proactive job seekers made simply by mustering the moxie to gain entrance to one of these huge events.

## *Once you're in the tradeshow:*

It takes a combination of professionalism, savvy and discretion to work the room once you gain access. Make sure you get a good night's rest the night before. Since companies are not there to find you, but to market to physicians and discuss the benefits of their products, their attention will be focused elsewhere.

However, as with all industry gatherings of this sort, there will be downtime for everyone. You'll need to use your best intuitive and perceptive skills to find the right moments to approach people and introduce yourself. These people work in the same "diplomatic" field and will take note of the way you conduct yourself.

To prepare, here's an important strategy. Get a list of all the companies in attendance along with a map of where each one will be setting up a booth. This information is usually listed on the websites for either the convention center (see page 74) or the healthcare conference. Draw up a "hit list" of your target companies. You'll want to visit their booths first. During the convention, once you approach a booth, hang back for a moment to observe what is happening before you enter the booth area. You'll want to try to identify who the key people are within the booth. If you can, start at the top and work your way down. Your goal is to speak with a director of sales, regional sales manager, district sales manager, senior sales representatives, hospital sales representatives or sales representatives.

When you see a lapse in foot traffic, and observe that your targeted contacts are not speaking with others, this is your moment to approach and introduce yourself. Right off the bat, tell them you realize they are very busy, but explain that you are interested in breaking into pharmaceutical sales with their company. Be confident, concise and focused. Make every second count because you may have only one or two before his or her attention is diverted. Ask if they are hiring. And, if so, see if you can leave a copy of your résumé for the hiring manager to review. Ask for a business card and find out if there is a best time or way for you to follow up later at a more convenient moment. Thank them for their time and, before leaving, reemphasize your strong interest in working for their company. Give them a firm handshake, make real eye contact and be on your way.

Immediately after leaving the booth, ideally once you are out of sight, stop and take notes on the business card of the person you just spoke with. These scrawled notations will be invaluable later in helping you remember the individual. Without them, you will be left with a stack of cards at day's end and, unless you have photographic recall, no clear recollection of the people they once belonged to.

For example, you might write, "Manager Carol Harris might have an opening coming up." Then, when you follow up via email, you can specifically mention the conversation by saying, "When we met you mentioned that Carol Harris might have an opening. Might you be able to give me Ms. Harris' email so that I can inquire and see if she does?" You can also record memorable personal data like, "Went to Syracuse University. Married. Two children. College football fan." Remembering those personal details will help you establish a bond with them. People will appreciate the fact that you took the time and care to remember something that is important to them.

When you follow up with an email, you might end the message with something like this, "Since you're a fan of Syracuse football, I thought you would appreciate this article from yesterday's *New York Times* on the prospects for this season." Then attach the article to the email.

As you can imagine, this sort of creative follow-up is effective in so many different contexts.

Managers I speak with tell me they admire a candidate who uses strategies of this sort because it speaks to their creativity, initiative and self-confidence. If you're unused to communicating with people you've just met in this manner, it may take some getting used to. But you'll get the hang of it — and even come to enjoy it — pretty quickly.

If you take all these steps, your network will grow quickly. Believe it or not, pretty soon you will have hundreds of business cards. If you take good notes, and enter your main contacts into a job search journal or digital assistant, it will help you tremendously.

Learn more about different conventions at these websites:

www.medicalconferences.com
www.bhpremiere.com
www.visitamerica.com/news/p_conventions.htm
www.aafp.org (go to CME, then Annual Meetings)
www.im.org/AAIM/ (look for conferences under "Events")

# NETWORKING — Job Fairs

Statistically, job fairs are not always the best use of your time, but they are worth attending because you never know where you will meet that one key contact. When researching which job fairs to attend, make sure to find out if pharmaceutical companies will be attending. Job fairs usually advertise in the Sunday newspaper Classified Jobs sections and on online job boards like Monster, Hotjobs and Medzilla, so look for them there.

The best thing you can do is contact the job fair company directly and ask the question. If any are scheduled to come, make sure they are companies that interest you. If there are several, make up a list the night before and write down a strategy for the day. To start with, show up before the doors open, and scope out where all the pharmaceutical company booths are located right away. Get into line quickly. As the day progresses, the lines will grow in front of the pharmaceutical companies — strong visual evidence of the competitive market for careers in pharmaceutical sales. At job fairs I've attended, the lines at the pharmaceutical company booths were anywhere from 10 to 15 times longer than the lines for all the others. As the day drags on, managers and sales representatives will droop. They become overwhelmed talking to so many people at once. That's why it is so important to make your appearance at the earliest possible moment.

I don't think I need to repeat this, but just in case: get business cards from everyone you meet. Take notes. Add them to your database.

When you follow up with them later, you will need to make reference to something brief and specific that will jog their memory of you. Work on your 30-second sales pitch by standing in front of a mirror and rehearsing. This will feel strange at first, but it works. You'll notice if you have any strange ticks or mannerisms (frowning when you don't mean to, breaking eye contact, biting your lip, etc.) that you'll want to eliminate. Robbie Evans, from Sanofi-Aventis, says this is one of the best pieces of advice he's ever received: "When you look in the mirror, you have a better understanding of how you come across to a district manager." You'll also get a chance to practice your language over and over again, syncing it with your physical presentation. Other people I know use a tape recorder and listen to their voice to work on establishing the best rhythm and to ensure they aren't speaking too slowly or too quickly.

There are some drawbacks to job fairs that you should be aware of before attending.

## Job Fair Drawbacks

- Long lines.
- Trying to distinguish yourself from hundreds of competitors.
- Companies sometimes use job fairs to replenish their reserve pool of candidates, but don't use them as a primary source of immediate hires.
- Companies may use job fairs as a means of keeping their names in the public spotlight.
- Even when job fair operators list pharmaceutical companies on their attendance rolls, they do not always attend.

For all these reasons, job fairs may not be the best use of your time. However, my friend Jennifer, the former sales recruiter from Johnson & Johnson, surprised me by reporting that she used to fill up to 20% of her open positions through individuals she met at job fairs. "The impact of a face-to-face meeting is so significant," she says.

Jennifer recommends that when you meet recruiters at job fairs, you should be prepared to run through a mini-interview in the space of just a few minutes. Be concise. Maintain eye contact. And make sure to close before saying goodbye. The close is so important that I've devoted all of Chapter 13 to the subject.

To learn more about job fairs, go to the following websites:

www.careerbuilder.com/jobseeker/careerfairs/
www.diversitycareergroup.com
www.hirehealth.com
www.hirequest.com
www.jobexpo.com
www.jobfairdirectory.com
www.job-hunt.org/fairs.shtml
http://content.monster.com/job-fairs/
www.salestrax.com
www.targetedjobfairs.com

## NETWORKING — Trade Magazines

Page through these industry publications to get a good overview of which companies are hiring and to stay up on industry trends. You might want to clip and mail articles to contacts you've met as a means of staying in touch.

We make great use of the following two industry magazines, sending articles to candidates and clients alike.

1) *Pharmaceutical Executive* magazine: www.pharmexec.com/pharmexec/

2) *Pharmaceutical Representative* magazine: www.pharmrep.com/pharmrep/

# NETWORKING — Newspaper Classified Advertisements

It's a long shot, but perusing the Sunday Classifieds will take only ten minutes. Pharmaceutical companies do post listings for openings. Along with job openings, you will stumble upon upcoming job fairs. Again, you never know where you'll turn up that one key contact.

# NETWORKING — Books and Directories

Many books of varying styles and quality have been written about pharmaceutical sales. One I recommend is written by Anne Clayton. It is rich in detail and research about the industry itself. If you want more in-depth macroeconomic research, read her book, *Insight Into a Career In Pharmaceutical Sales.*

## TOM'S TIP — REMEMBER MY NAME

DALE CARNEGIE FAMOUSLY SAID that the sweetest sound to any person is the sound of his or her own name. When I heard this, it struck a chord in me. Think of how great it feels when you meet somebody for only the second time and they remember to greet you by name. I am, well, kind of fanatical about recording names of all of the people in my life: friends, friends of friends, all business associates (I really mean all), people at my favorite restaurants, doormen, the woman behind the counter at my dry cleaner and my mailman.

YOU MAY THINK I'M EXAGGERATING, BUT I'M NOT.

REMEMBERING PEOPLES' NAMES will set you apart in your hunt for your first job in pharmaceutical sales. If you follow all the guidelines in this book, believe me, you will be meeting a lot of people. Now, your task is to remember ALL of their names.

This habit will serve you well once you're on the job, too. You can only ask a particular client his or her name so many times. After the second or third time, people will be put off.

I store names in the TREO PDA I carry with me at all times. I trust nothing to my memory. I type notes about their appearances to help recall their faces to my mind. Successful job candidates I know took notes in their daily planners as they went on interviews. Write names down on the back of a receipt if you must. There's no better way to start an interview than with eye contact, a strong handshake and a confident greeting — beginning with your interviewer's first name.

## CHAPTER SIX

# Interview Preparation – Everything You Need

" Pressure comes when someone calls on you to perform
a task for which you are not prepared. "

— Tony LaRussa, Head Coach,  2006 World Champion
St. Louis Cardinals Baseball team

# Checklist

For each interview with a prospective employer, you should already have studied the company along the guidelines laid out in Chapter Four. Take this research and assemble the most important points onto 3 × 5-inch flash cards. Keep these with you and start going through them days before the interview, whether it is occurring in person or over the phone. Continue to do so the night before and the morning of. When you get your body involved (by shuffling those cards), you're more likely to retain the information on them. The cards should include:

1) A list of new product launches and the amount of money allocated for research and development (from the Company Profiles section of this book and/or the company website). You can break out the products onto separate flash cards.

2) Information from a Hoover's profile on the company (hoovers.com).

3) The number of employees in the company versus the number of sales representatives.

4) A Top Ten list of the reasons you want to work for this particular company (see page 83).

5) A Top Ten list of the reasons why this company should hire you (see page 83).

6) A list of questions to ask your interviewer (see page 127).

7) Write out the top ten most likely questions (see page 122 for a sample). Write out your responses and role-play them over and over again.

# The Night Before

The night before the interview, go through the following checklist to make sure you have everything you need:

1) Multiple copies of your brag book with a personalized cover page that includes the company name and the hiring manager's name on the front.

2) Clear directions to the interview. If you are interviewing in a corporate office, contact the office manager or receptionist to get accurate driving directions. If you aren't familiar with the area, drive to the interview location the day before your interview so you don't get lost when it counts. This also eliminates unwanted stress on the day of the interview and allows you to focus on the task at hand: nailing the interview.

3) Suit set out, shirt pressed and shoes shined.

4) All of your research done and a one-page summary of the steps you've taken to prepare for the interview (see below).

5) Full tank of gas in your car. You don't want to risk dirtying your suit pumping gas on the day of the interview.

6) Send an email confirmation to the interviewer the day before the interview. This is a courtesy that demonstrates your thoroughness and professionalism. Keep it short and concise.

## Sample Interview Confirmation Email:

Dear (hiring manager),

This email is to confirm our interview tomorrow, Monday, June 5 at 8:00 a.m. at your Regional Office at 123 Main Street.

I have been doing extensive research into your company and products. I am excited about this opportunity and I look forward to meeting you tomorrow morning.

Sincerely,

Your Name

# ABC Company Interview Preparation and Research

- Reviewed corporate website.
- Subscribed to ABC Company's presentation, calendar and financial release email notification service.
- Contacted current office managers outside the state to ask questions about their knowledge of and experience with ABC Company. Learned about how they work with physicians' offices.
- Called customer service and inquired about XYZ drug.
- Reviewed annual report presentation; I noted an increase in sales of XYZ drug over the previous two fiscal years.
- Investigated the population of doctors' offices in the West Los Angeles territory and collected contact information.
- Constructed a 30/60/90 day action plan for the West Los Angeles territory.
- Educated myself about the flow and sales protocol of doctors' offices.
- Interviewed two separate office managers regarding their views on dealing with sales representatives and with ABC Company.

# Preparation

### *Top Ten Reasons Why They Should Hire You and Why You Want to Work for This Company*

Your Top Ten lists should be tailored specifically to the company and, if this is a follow-up interview, to your experience with your interviewer(s). You can insert these lists in your brag book. Later, I'll show you how to use them a second time, as part of a creative follow-up to your interview. Here are successful Top Ten formats.

# Top Ten Reasons Why ABC Pharmaceuticals Should Hire Me

1. My professionalism and high level of integrity.
2. My thorough understanding of ABC Pharmaceuticals' products.
3. My passion for the industry.
4. My successful experience working on teams.
5. My networking capabilities.
6. My strong interpersonal skills and my ability to "read" another person.
7. My honesty and high ethical standards.
8. My listening skills.
9. My competitive nature.
10. My familiarity with the sales territory.

Plus ...

- I want the position more than anyone else!

# Top Ten Reasons Why I Want to work for ABC Pharmaceuticals

1. ABC Pharmaceuticals was named the best-managed company in the drug and biotechnology industry this year.
2. ABC Pharmaceuticals has appeared on the Forbes Platinum list of the 400 best companies in America for the last three years.
3. ABC Pharmaceuticals is one of the fastest-growing companies in the industry.
4. The people at ABC Pharmaceuticals believe in the power of potential.
5. ABC Pharmaceuticals offers a solid product portfolio; its newest product, Medicine 1, is a potential blockbuster.

6. ABC Pharmaceuticals is built on integrity.

7. ABC Pharmaceuticals is deeply committed to its employees.

8. ABC Pharmaceuticals anticipates steady growth in its product pipeline, revenues and workforce.

9. I was impressed with the professionalism and sincerity of my interviewer, John Doe.

10. Every physician, pharmacist and patient I have spoken with speaks highly of ABC Pharmaceuticals' products.

# Attire

Before you arrive at your first in-person interview, before you open your mouth and sometimes even before you approach your interviewer, you may already have created a make-or-break impression. You must look the part. If you don't, no matter how thorough your research, none of it will matter.

I know what you are saying right now, "Anyone knows how to dress for an interview." Think again. You may not. I am still amazed that people don't spend more time on their appearance and grooming. On the surface, appearance sounds like a superficial subject. In a sales job, it isn't. A well-groomed, appropriately-attired job candidate is someone who has taken time and care, and invested resources, in preparing to dress for the job. With good reason, district managers will make decisions based in part on your personal appearance. If you want more insight into just why, read *Blink*, another book by author Malcolm Gladwell. People can't help it. In so many areas of human life, we rely on snap decisions — even when we think we don't. Put this human reflex to work in your favor by adequately preparing and following these guidelines.

## *Proper attire for Men:*

- Navy blue or black, single-breasted suit (slacks and a sport coat are *not* acceptable)
- Crisp, white dress shirt, heavy starch
- Conservative, sturdy tie

- Black wing tip shoes, freshly shined before every interview
- Matching color socks, close in tone to the fabric of your suit
- Little or no jewelry (lose the earrings, gold chains, bracelet or pinky ring)
- Little or no cologne
- Hair neatly groomed
- Clean fingernails (we know a candidate who was not hired for this reason alone)

## *Appropriate attire for women:*

- Navy blue or black conservative suit, or
- Pant or skirt suit
- White blouse
- Shined shoes
- Limited jewelry
- No dangling earrings
- Little or no perfume
- Hair professionally styled or pulled back
- Clean fingernails

A note on the white shirt. For men, in particular, wearing a white shirt is the safest route. As my friend Lou says, "It's not a written policy, but it's an old-school pharmaceutical thing."

# CHAPTER SEVEN

## The Ride-Along

**"**Familiarity breeds contempt, while rarity wins admiration.**"**

— Apuleius

If a prospective employer is serious about you, you will be asked to accompany a working sales representative on a ride-along. If you've done one beforehand, as part of your research, you will have a good sense of what to expect. During a formal ride-along, as part of the interview process, you will usually spend an entire day in the field.

*The purpose of the ride-along is twofold: the company gets to know you better and you get an education about the particular demands of the job.*

Having a working representative spend an entire day with you gives him or her a sense of you as a person. You will be observed interacting with customers and a pharmaceutical representative will also closely observe how you interact with him or her. Importantly, the sales representative is looking for a window into your "true" self. There will be many opportunities starting over breakfast, during morning sales calls, over lunch and during the hours spent together driving in a car. The most important piece of advice I can give you here is not to let your guard down. No matter how much time you spend with one another, remember that you are in an interview situation the entire time.

My good friend Heidi-Anne Mooney, a former senior sales representative with Abbott Laboratories, was once told by a 23-year industry veteran that, in college, doctors learned from professors who wore lab coats or suits. "So if you want to walk into a doctor's office and sell them a product or teach them about a new product," Heidi-Anne says, "dress like their professors did. They will be more apt to take you seriously. I always thought this was smart advice." Yet another reason to take care with your appearance.

At the beginning of the day, you need to ask the representative what the protocol for the day will be. In other words, how does he or she expect you to behave? This is a crucial step. Each representative will observe different rules of etiquette. One will want you to shadow and say little to customers beyond the initial salutation and exchange of good-byes. Others will permit, or even expect, you to interject a comment here and there to see how you might handle a sales call on your own. A failure to discuss protocol can spell the end of your chances with this representative's company. We've often fielded calls from aggravated sales representatives who complain to us about the behavior or misbehavior of a job candidate who, it later emerged, was simply unclear about the representative's expectations for his or her behavior. Don't set yourself up to fail by skipping this conversation.

Be alert to the probability that the representative may use a ploy, similar to that of a district manager during your interview, of putting you at ease to see how you will behave. Quite often, he or she will offer you opportunities to discuss personal matters to see whether you end up revealing more than you should. One of our candidates relaxed so thoroughly during a ride-along that he began telling the representative stories about nightclubbing and staying out late and drinking. To him, it felt like a bonding moment. He was surprised to learn that the representative called the district manager and advised her not to hire this individual. He was described as being stuck in a post-collegiate "party mode," which indicated a lack of seriousness. You've probably surmised he didn't get the job.

Here is Heidi-Anne Mooney talking about some of her experiences over the course of many years taking job candidates on ride-alongs:

> One gentleman I interviewed was dying to get into pharmaceutical sales. He was nice and seemed smart, but he kept calling all the front office receptionists or back medical assistants "hon," "honey" or "dude." He also wore Dockers and a short sleeve business shirt. These were red flags for my district manager. Another gentleman kept asking how much money we got to entertain doctors for golf.

An avid golfer, he really wanted this job so he could golf a lot. Over the course of the day, he only asked me questions about golf. Another lady I interviewed was fresh out of college and determined to break into this industry, but she had poor spatial awareness and kept getting in the way of the back office staff. She wouldn't move aside when a patient came down the hallway with a nurse, or she'd pick up medical charts in the back and flip through them, disrespecting the office's privacy. These seemingly little nuisances became glaring when I compared these candidates to their competitors and reported back to my district manager.

Behaving with exceptional sensitivity in doctors' offices is more important now than ever. With so many pharmaceutical sales representatives competing for their attention, some doctors have limited their time with each to only 90 seconds, according to a recent story in *Business Week*. The margin for unprofessional behavior has reduced to close to zero.

The second component of the ride-along is that it is for your own benefit. The company wants you to experience firsthand a day in the life of one of their pharmaceutical representatives so that you have a clear sense of the job. If a company does not offer you a ride-along as part of the interview process, ask for one yourself, for your own benefit. Even a half-day ride-along is better than none. This will be a good way for you to make sure that this is a company you would like to work for.

As the day unfolds, take fastidious notes between sales calls. You will want to record which offices you called upon, the names of products you discussed, the doctors' names, all the issues that came up, any customer complaints and how the representative handled them. Ask the representative how he or she targets the business and measures success. You will use these notes to prepare a ride-along summary to email to the district manager the very same day as your ride-along. This will reinforce your education that day and, again, demonstrate your attention to detail and ability to work quickly.

Throughout the day, you will want to ask the representative a series of questions.

# Ride-along questions for the representative

- What do you like and dislike about your job?
- What are the biggest challenges you are currently facing?
- What is the district manager's management style?
- Have you worked for other pharmaceutical companies? (If so) How does your current district manager compare to your past ones?
- What is the company culture like?
- How do you target your business and measure success?
- Can you tell me about any current selling programs at your company?
- What general advice do you have for me?
- What are the best steps I can take to secure this job?

At the end of the day, you will need to "close" in the same way you would with a doctor, with a district manager during an in-person interview, with a district manager at the end of a phone interview or in a super-short conversation you would have with a hiring manager at a job fair or trade show. I cannot overemphasize the importance of the close. If you fail to close, you will fail to get the job. It's as simple as that. I've devoted Chapter 13 to the subject. Here is a script you may choose to use at the end of your ride-along.

# The Ride-Along Close:

"I appreciate your time and input today. You have been a great resource. You've given me a better understanding of what to expect in this job. You validated much of my research, but seeing the job up close has only increased my desire for the position. After spending a day in the field with me and learning about my background, do you have any reservations or concerns that would prevent you from recommending me for this position?" *If the answer is yes, make sure to listen to those concerns and fully address them before continuing along the following lines:* "Before I leave you today, I want you to know I want this job! Based on my five years of successful outside sales experience, my strong understanding of the clinical side of the business and my overall desire to succeed, I am confident I will be a valuable asset to your company. *What do I need to do to get this job?" Here, say absolutely nothing. Wait for a response. Then add*, "Do I have your recommendation?" *Again, say absolutely nothing and listen.*

After your impassioned close, request a business card from the representative and make sure to send him or her a handwritten thank-you note, as well as another thank-you via email. Also send your district manager your summary of what you learned and observed during the ride-along. It's important to email it that very night.

The following is an actual ride-along summary sent by one of our successful candidates to a district manager of a large pharmaceutical company. The candidate included a cover letter with her overall observations about the experience and a strong reiteration of her interest in the position. The names of individuals, companies and medications have been changed.

# Sample Ride-Along Summary

## Korea town

8:00 a.m. — Met with Paula Katz at Starbucks on Wilshire and Main St. Discussed her position and how she operates in her territory.

8:45 a.m. — Went to a Korean bakery and picked up two boxes of bread for clients.

9:05 a.m. — Dr. John Mao — (This doctor is one of Paula's high-volume doctors. She visits him twice a week at the very least).
- Reviewed pre-call data and product spreadsheets.
- Refilled samples of Medicine 1 in his clinic.
- Competitively sold Medicine 1 over Competing Medicine 2, talked about Competing Medicine 3's horrible side effects (51% interest level — Paula asked him a lead-in question, an option A or an option B. He was focused on

what he was doing and only responded with a yes, which did not answer our question.)

- Confirmed dinner for Friday. (He seemed busy. We anticipated Paula would have more time to discuss product differentiation over dinner.)
- Dr. Mao received a phone call from a representative from a Competing Pharmaceutical Company while we were there.

9:25 a.m. — Called on pharmacy in the building. Asked the pharmacist which prescriptions he writes. He writes Medicine 1 for HP and Respiratory.

9:35 a.m. — Logged in post-call data and entered follow-up information for Dr. Mao.

9:45 a.m. — Dr. John Tan
- Reviewed pre-call data and product spreadsheets.
- We also saw Dr. Martin Peterson, who we know is Dr. Tan's go-to guy for his patients' G.I. problems. Talked to Dr. Peterson about his vacation and about Medicine 3.
- Competitively sold against Competing Medicine 4 (attentive — 85% interest level).
- Closed for specific Bluecross and MediCal business.
- Dropped off pastry.

10:00 a.m. — Logged post-call data. Closed Dr. Tan on Rx to Medicine 3.

10:10 a.m. — Dr. Bob Jung
- Refilled samples on Medicine 2 at Dr. Jung's office.
- Talked to the gatekeeper.

10:26 a.m. — Dr. Ed Song
- Reviewed pre-call data and product spreadsheets.
- Dropped off pastry.

- Competitively sold against Competing Medicine 3. He said he writes Competing Medicine 3 because it came out before Medicine 2, and he has never had a problem with the product.
- Confirmed dinner on Thursday.

10:45 a.m. — Logged post-call data. Entered follow-up information for Dr. Song.

## Chinatown

11:15 a.m. — Dr. Carl Wong
- Reviewed pre-call data and product spreadsheets.
- Competitively sold against Competing Medicine 3 and determined which prescriptions he is writing.
- The gatekeeper said he was busy and would be available after 3 p.m.

11:30 a.m. — Dr. Norman See
- Reviewed pre-call data and product spreadsheets.
- Competitively sold against Competing Medicine 2. (Attentive — 85% interest level)

11:50 a.m. — Dr. Chung Ho
- Refilled Medicine 2.

12:00 p.m. — Called on College Pharmacy in Dr. Ho's building.

12:10 p.m. — Logged post-call data. Entered follow-up information for Drs. Ho and See.

12:30 p.m. — Dr. Rufus Chin
- Reviewed pre-call data and product spreadsheets.
- Refilled Medicine 1.

1:00 p.m. — Dr. Bob Kwan (This doctor is one of Paula's high-volume doctors. She visits him twice a week at the very least).

- Lunch.
- Patricia Woo met with us at the luncheon at Dr. Kwan's office.
- Discussed interest in other products as opposed to Competing Medicine 2.
  (Attentive — 90% interest level)

2:20 p.m.–2:45 p.m. — Reviewed the day up to that point and discussed my questions about the field.

## Little Tokyo

3:00 p.m. — Dr. Hiroshi Mitamura
- Reviewed pre-call data and product spreadsheets.
- Talked about Medicine 1 and clarified any questions the doctor had in regards to the product. (Attentive — 85% interest level)

4:00 p.m. — Dr. Koji Kita
- Talked to him about Medicine 1 and his interests. (Very attentive — 95% interest level)

5:00 p.m. — Logged post-call data and entered information to follow up on for Drs. Mitamura and Kita.

5:10 p.m. — Recapped at end of the day.

## CHAPTER EIGHT

# The Interview — How to Sell

**❝** In selling, as in medicine, prescription
before diagnosis is malpractice. **❞**

— Tony Alessandra

D ays or weeks beforehand, begin role-playing the subjects you will be asked to cover during an interview. Some of the best salespeople I know make a point about role-playing selling scenarios before they "perform" them for a customer — or an interviewer. At some point in your interview, you will be asked to sell your interviewer something. It could be a pen, a wallet or yourself. In selling, unlike many other things in life, there is a right way and a wrong way to do it. Through this exercise, your interviewer is trying to determine whether or not you have been trained in the art. If you stumble here, you won't get the job. This may sound challenging, but it's a learned skill. Once you've got some coaching, it's a breeze, even fun.

One of the best books on this form of selling is *Spin Selling* by Neil Rackham. It's a favorite of one of the best salespeople I've ever met, my friend Brett Butler, the president of Document Consulting Services Inc., a premier Xerox sales agency in El Segundo, California. Brett is a master among masters; the Xerox sales training program is the gold standard, and the company trains many people who go on to successful sales careers in every other industry.

A highly-trained salesperson, as Brett explains it, goes through seven steps in order to effectively sell anything. These are:

| | | | | |
|---|---|---|---|---|
| 1. | Fact Find | | 5. | Recommend |
| 2. | Probe | | 6. | Close |
| 3. | Agree | | 7. | Follow-up |
| 4. | Influence | | | |

If your interviewer hands you a pen and asks you to sell it back to her, the first thing you should do is set that pen aside. Even put it out of sight. You begin by asking a series of "fact-finding" questions. This is a role-play so, to some extent, you can invent details. You might ask, "How many pens does your company buy a year? For how many locations?" And then, "Who aside from you will be making the eventual buying decisions?" You want to ascertain whether you're speaking with a gatekeeper or a decision maker.

Once you know your audience, begin to probe: "What sorts of problems are you having right now with the pens you are buying?" Make sure to magnify the problem when you figure out what it is; tie it to larger business strategies: "So when your sales force complains that their pens don't work, do you transact less business?"

Then, again, magnify the pain: "And how much does that cost?"

During this process, Brett says, "Over and over and over again, you shed light on the pain until the customer realizes he or she is bleeding and in need of a bandage."

You want to discover the problem, very specifically, tie it to the relevant larger issues and then ask what this person would like to do to find a solution.

Finally you are ready to ask, "Do you agree that you have to make a change?" If so, move forward. If not, don't invest any more energy. You're not working with a viable customer. If the person is undecided, go back and scratch some more to help further identify and magnify the pain to understand and illustrate its impact. You might ask, "How does malfunctioning equipment affect the morale of your people?"

Once you've got agreement, it's time to influence. Here the ground has been laid. You recap all the unique qualities of your particular product — your pen — and describe how it will improve your prospective client's business. "You set up a list of requirements that the customer will buy into," Brett says. For the purposes of a role-play, it's O.K. to fabricate features (although not if you're role-playing the sale of an actual medicine). You might say, "Our pen has a pressurized cartridge that will allow your salespeople to write out their order forms on a vertical wall without the ink drying out."

Next you recommend the product. You're getting ready to close, but you must make sure you've earned it before you begin. When you do close, you are asking for a specific commitment to buy, perhaps a dollar amount or a quantity. "For a person who has done a great job at fact-finding, probing and getting the customer to agree that they need to make a change, the close should be automatic," Brett says. After securing a commitment to buy and signing documents, sketch out a follow-up. You might say that you will pay this customer a return visit in three days to check on the order status and to make sure she is happy with her purchase. "You want to create the perception that this is not a one-time sale, but the start of a relationship," Brett says.

It's a cliché, but good selling is truly an art. Great sales people relish this part of the job. In a sense, they are performers. Take the time to practice — to role-play — your performances before the interview, even if it is only with an imaginary interviewer. Don't "rehearse" on a district manager or you're likely to flub your lines and blow the audition.

The following is a sample script that roughly follows the seven stages of selling mentioned before and is tailored to the pharmaceutical sales call or — as it is also known in the industry — the "detail." It contains more information than you are likely to need in an interview setting, but if you study this entire script, you will have a clear sense of how working representatives sell to doctors on the job.

# The Representative's "Detail" (sales call) to a doctor

## 1) Opening

Begin your detail talking about the patients. Paint a picture of the target patient type based on symptoms. When the doctor encounters such a patient, he will think of you, the medicine you discussed and the commitments he made to you at the end of the call.

*Sample script:* "Doctor, in your waiting room, I saw a few patients with red eyes and runny noses, who may be suffering from asthma-related symptoms due to the peak ragwood season."

## 2) Opening Question and Probing

Once you've opened the topic, probe for information to understand how the doctor derives an algorithm to treat asthma and/or write prescriptions.

*Sample script:* "When patients come in during ragweed season complaining of symptoms, what is the first thing you look for in formulating a diagnosis and planning your prescription protocol?"

You may need to visit this doctor three or four times to extract one or two tidbits of information to help you understand exactly how this doctor approaches the treatment of this disease state. Once you've accomplished this, discuss the benefits of your product.

*Sample question:* "What do you think of the American Academy of Allergy guidelines? Do you follow these guidelines when treating patients with asthma-related symptoms or are there other guidelines you prefer?"

## 3) Support Benefits

To outline the benefits, give the doctor a supporting medical reprint from a well-known medical journal that is approved by your company.

Throughout your entire detail, take frequent mental "pulse checks" of the doctor. Is she mentally focused on what you are saying or already thinking about the next patient? Look for body language. Does she look interested in what you are saying? Are her arms crossed in a confrontational manner? If so, this may be a good time to offer a medical reprint to help loosen her up. If she seems busy or disinterested, you can acknowledge this and suggest that you return at a later time to discuss the matter. Doctors will appreciate this insight and courtesy on your part. While you relinquish the chance of making a sale that day, you're better positioned to make one later and to build a long-term relationship. You won't help your case by annoying a doctor.

## 4) Know Your Competition

Be prepared to discuss your competitors' products, including similar features and benefits as well as downfalls. Even if you are selling a "me-too" drug (one similar to others on the market), yours may be less expensive or come with better formulary coverage.

## 5) Handle Obstacles or Objections

Rehearse ahead of time so that you are prepared to respond appropriately to any obstacles or objections the doctor may raise.

*Sample script:* "Doctor, I understand you like Medicine B due to the formulary coverage and how easy it is for your patients to take, but you may be surprised to hear that Medicine A has recently been added to the American Academy of Allergy recommendations. Here are the latest AAA guidelines published just this month. In fact, in a head-to-head study quoted here, Medicine A had three times fewer side effects than Medicine B. It also costs $30.00 less per month for the formularies than Medicine B."

One important note: when a doctor brings up an objection, never tell him he is wrong. Or — as we say in the industry — never call the doctor's baby ugly. If he has a product (his baby) that he frequently prescribes, do not put that product down directly. Instead, illustrate how your drug may offer a better alternative. Doing this without causing offense is a learned skill that, with practice, you will master over time.

## 6) Setup to Close

*Sample script:* "Doctor, have I provided you with enough information so that you now can feel confident about prescribing Medicine A as opposed to Medicine B?"

If not, respond to his concerns.

## 7) Discuss Formulary Status

No drug is covered everywhere. You'll need to have your company's charts with you to show how well your product is covered and to be able to explain to your doctor which health plans he can use to prescribe it. Make sure that before you go on the call you know which health plans cover this care. Each company provides this data. There's nothing more frustrating than making a sale only to discover that your drug isn't covered by any of the doctor's health plans.

## 8) Close

*Sample script:* "Is it fair for me to ask you to try Medicine A today for the next patient that you see suffering from asthma-related symptoms brought on by ragweed?"

## 9) Discuss Methods of Prescription and Dosages

Once you have secured the doctor's commitment to prescribe, remind him or her how to write the prescription and at what dosages. Be sure, also, to mention possible side effects. This will show fair balance of how your product might work compared to another. It will also, most importantly, prepare him in case patients call back with side effects.

In some cases you may want to draw a contrast with a specific medication.

*Sample script:* "I know that Medicine B (the drug the doctor most frequently prescribes) is a great drug because it's been around for 15 years and has been considered the gold standard in treating asthma symptoms, but Medicine A (your product) causes half the symptoms of stomach upset in head-to-head trials. Medicine A also comes in a smaller pill, which is easier to swallow. It need be taken only once a day and costs $10 less than Medicine B for your patients who pay cash for their prescriptions."

## 10) Follow up

Once a doctor commits to trying your product, it is imperative that you follow up and hold her to that commitment. Say, for example, she agreed to try Medicine A instead of Medicine B for the next asthma patient she sees. You or a counterpart need to follow up within two to three days to see if she has followed through. If you wait until your next visit to the office, her promise may be a distant memory. So, let the doctor know you will check back in on her, and then do.

## CHAPTER NINE

# The Phone Interview

❝ You can have anything you want if you want it desperately enough. You must want it with an inner exuberance that erupts through the skin and joins the energy that created the world. ❞

— Sheila Graham

Before you make it to an in-person interview, you may be required to clear the hurdle of the phone interview. This can be tricky without the right preparation and strategy. The challenge lies in trying to understand the interviewer since you can't observe body language or facial expressions over the phone. Of the ten elements of a successful phone interview, the first two are the most important.

## *Keys to a Successful Phone Interview*

1. **Treat the phone interview like a regular interview. It is.**
   If you don't pass the phone interview, that's it. You've lost your opportunity to proceed. Candidates often don't prepare thoroughly for the phone interview because they don't take it as seriously as an in-person meeting. This is a mistake! Managers who reject candidates after the phone interview commonly complain that the candidate was either ill-prepared or simply not compelling enough to meet in person. You must be prepared, you must have a good story to tell, and you need to close the interviewer in order to move to the next step. (More on closing in Chapter 13.) The object of your phone interview is to move to the next step: the in-person interview.

2. **Stand up and walk around when you are talking on the phone.**
   This movement increases the blood flow, which increases your energy level. This also allows your voice to project in a clear and confident manner. Ninety percent of the time I am on the phone, I

am standing or walking around. I have a wireless headset so I pace the room, wave my hands and talk in an animated manner. All this energy translates across the phone line to the other person. Have a trusted friend ask you interview questions over the phone so you can rehearse your answers with your résumé on the table in front of you. Also, ask that friend to help you test your handset or headset's reception at varying distances from the base set.

3. **Wear a suit.** Some candidates find dressing the part helps them to act it.

4. **Have your résumé and brag book in front of you.** Be prepared to discuss every single item on them, including dates of employment, time gaps, promotions and every single number.

5. **Secure a quiet place where you have privacy.** Ideally, call from a landline for the interview versus a cell phone to avoid static or a dropped call. If you have no other option than to use a cell phone, be sure to find a quiet spot with a strong cell signal.

6. **Don't forget to smile!** That's right. Smile, even though you are not looking right at someone's face. Smiling comes through over the phone. Your interviewer wants to hear a confident, happy and friendly voice. You can convey that if you smile. Some people look into a mirror while they talk to ensure that they do. Radio stations hire announcers who convey a "smile in the voice." Put one in yours.

7. **Ask the same questions you would ask in an in-person interview** (See page 127 for examples): What are you looking for in an individual? What is the biggest challenge you are currently facing in this territory? Why is the territory open?

8. **Ask a question.** If your interviewer seems to lose focus (he or she might decide to send an email, for example), ask a question to bring them back to re-energize the conversation.

9. **As I've mentioned, it's crucial that you close the interview strongly.** I explore closing in greater detail in Chapter 13, but you'll want to end the conversation with a question like this: "After talking to me on the phone and reviewing my background, do you have any reservations or concerns that would prevent you from bringing me in for a face-to-face interview?" If there are concerns, address them, repeat the question and then ask when you might be able to come in for a follow-up interview.

10. Before ending the phone call, request your interviewer's email address so you can send an email thanking him or her for taking the time to speak with you.

*Remember, you have one objective:* To go from a telephone interview to a face-to-face meeting. Take the phone interview as seriously as any other.

## CHAPTER TEN

# The In-Person Interview

❝ All your life they will say you're not good enough or strong enough or talented enough; they will say you're the wrong height or the wrong weight or the wrong type to play this or be this or achieve this. THEY WILL TELL YOU NO, a thousand times no, until all the nos become meaningless.... AND YOU WILL TELL THEM YES. ❞

**— Nike**

You've taken all the necessary steps to prepare for this moment. You've created a brag book, researched the company, talked to people within the organization, dressed appropriately, gotten a haircut, shined your shoes, clipped your fingernails and brushed your teeth. So, here goes…

One of my friends, Jonathan Siade-Cox, a former district manager for Johnson & Johnson (pharmaceuticals), who is now with a large biotech concern, tells me he decides within two to three minutes whether or not to hire a candidate. He is not alone. Various studies have shown that most hiring decisions are made about that quickly. In some cases, it happens earlier; if you're spotted in the hotel lobby beforehand dressed inappropriately or behaving unprofessionally, you can lose your chance even before hello. If you've followed all the guidelines I've laid out thus far, you've improved your odds of success.

Here's something else that will help: you will endear yourself to every interviewer if you keep in mind something that Calvin, from the comic strip *Calvin & Hobbes*, once said, "If something is so complicated that you can't explain it in 10 seconds, then it's probably not worth knowing anyway." In other words, keep it simple.

## The First Question

By telephone or in person, the first question you'll probably be asked is the most obvious one: "Why do you want to get into pharmaceutical sales?" It's what most district managers want to know at the outset. It's the first thing I ask candidates I may choose to represent. Very quickly

— sometimes right away — I will be able to tell whether I'm speaking with a viable candidate. I cringe when I hear the following answers.

## How *not* to respond

- I have friends in the industry.
- I hear it's a lot of fun.
- I hear you can make a ton of money.
- Free company car.
- Flexible hours.
- Golf.

While these may be legitimate reasons, they don't cut it with companies. Lead with these answers and a district manager is likely to end the interview rather quickly. You will have revealed yourself as someone who doesn't have a serious grasp of what the job entails. As you already know, research is the key factor in readying yourself for the interview.

If you have followed even a fraction of the advice laid out in the preceding chapters, you will present a very different picture. Here's one version of a winning response to that question.

## What you should say when asked why you want the job:

"I've interviewed more than 20 pharmaceutical sales representatives and learned what they do to be successful. I've gone on three ride-alongs to get a street-level sense of the work involved. I've spoken with my physician to find out what she values in a pharmaceutical sales representative. I've obtained contact information for the top representatives she knows and have spoken with each of them directly. I've spent more hours than I can count researching the industry — and your own company. I've read three books on the subject, and I go through *The Wall Street Journal* daily to stay abreast of industry trends. All this footwork has convinced me that this is the right job for me and that I can make a real contribution at the right company."

Right away, you've set the tone for what will be a substantive interview. Everything you said, of course, had better be true because it will lead to the subjects you will discuss over the next hour. You'll need to elaborate on these experiences in great detail to demonstrate to your interviewer that you've absorbed all the lessons from them that you could.

# The Day Of

The morning of your interview make sure to eat a good breakfast with some protein. This may sound basic, but having a good — and sustained — energy level is key to a successful interview. Some candidates like to have a coffee or an espresso before an interview to give them a boost to their energy level. Others wouldn't dream of letting caffeine upset their equilibrium. Bottom line, whatever works for you to get you pumped up and in good spirits, go for it.

**No matter what, do not be late for an interview!** It makes a terrible — and often insurmountable — first impression and can prompt your elimination from the interview process before it even begins. One of our top clients, a Fortune 500 pharmaceutical company, will end an interview on the spot if a candidate is more than five minutes late. Another district manager friend tells me, "If they're late, they're done." Not all interviewers are so cut-and-dried, but you should assume they are. Sometimes circumstances beyond any human control do intervene. If the worst happens, and you know you are going to be delayed, call ahead and forewarn your interviewer. You may be able to salvage the interview.

When you do arrive, be early. Plan to be. After you get out of your car or off the train, walk around the interview location for a few minutes, take some deep breaths and unwind from your travel. This helps get the blood circulating and increases your energy level. Visualize the interview and imagine your best interview ever. Do a quick check of your appearance and make sure there are no breakfast stains on your tie or white blouse. If you are a coffee drinker, take a breath mint before you start the interview. There's nothing worse than being an interviewer in a small conference room with a candidate who has coffee breath or just plain bad breath (trust me — I know).

Ten to fifteen minutes before the scheduled start, head in and let them know you've arrived, providing the name of your interviewer.

To make a strong first impression, start with a firm, confident handshake and a warm smile. Maintain intense eye contact. Research has shown that the first 30 seconds make or break the connection between two people when they meet for the first time. Display continuous enthusiasm for the job throughout the interview. Sit up straight and on the edge of your chair — no slouching and certainly no chewing gum. Be attentive.

Great listening skills are important in an interview, as they will be on the job. Follow the two-second rule: wait two seconds before responding to the interviewer's question.

# The Two-Second Rule

This may feel counter-intuitive at first. Give yourself the chance to get used to doing so. Practice it with a friend in your role-play. It shows professionalism, respect and confidence. Don't jump on the tail end of your interviewer's sentences. While you may sound eager, you will not come off as polite or professional.

When answering questions be very concise and to the point, answer the question and then, stop! Say absolutely nothing. Don't ramble on and on. This is a common mistake and a mark of insecurity. You can ask if your interviewer would like you to expand on your answers, but it is wise not to do so without prompting. One to two minutes is the typical response time for more in-depth questions. Time yourself during your role-plays to see how long your answers run naturally.

# Beware

An interviewer may try to lull you off your game by behaving very casually. He or she may kick back in a chair and talk about very personal matters, in an off-handed way. Don't take this bait. Your discretion is being tested. Regardless of how comfortable you are with the interviewer, *always* keep your guard up and don't forget you are being scrutinized. At this time, in particular, it's easy to slip and say something negative about your current or a former employer. Don't do it. I recently interviewed three people for a position. Two criticized a former employer. You can guess which of the three I hired. **Under no circumstances should you ever make a negative comment about a current or former employer during the interview process.** If your interviewer becomes chummy, remember that you can still be friendly and build rapport without revealing too many details about your personal life or dropping your professionalism.

According to different studies by experts, non-verbal communication accounts for between 55% and 80% of information conveyed in any human interaction.

What does this mean to you? Even if you don't have the "cookie cutter" background, there is hope. You still have a good chance of having a successful interview based on how you come across. My best advice is that you have some fun, let your personality shine through, and realize that, if this is meant to be, it will all work out. While you can control your behavior, you cannot control how you will be perceived. Let this be a reason to relax. If the interview doesn't go well, this may be due to factors ranging from your interviewer's dental surgery to office politics. If you feel you could have done a better job yourself, put what you learn to good use in the next interview. Don't put so much pressure on yourself that you hurt your chances. Take a few deep breaths, stay focused and enjoy the experience.

## 1. Introduction and small talk

This is a chance for you to build rapport with the interviewer. Some interviewers want to see what type of a personality you have and how well you discuss non-work matters. This is an important skill to have in pharmaceutical sales. As a drug rep, you will find yourself spending a lot of time waiting for a doctor and talking to the office staff. Some district managers are looking for candidates with the gift of gab. But don't overdo it. Scientifically minded companies like Merck don't hire candidates who run at the mouth. Learn to strike the right balance. Read *The New York Times*, *The Wall Street Journal* and *USA Today* every day leading up to your interview and watch CNN Headline News the morning of for a brief overview of the current events of the day.

The interviewer will let you know when it's time to get started with the nitty-gritty of the interview, so if he or she opens the door to casual conversation, walk right on in. Sometimes a common interest will come up, such as a sports team or a book you've both read. This is a great chance to establish a connection.

## 2. Summarizing your résumé

You should really start to shine when the interviewer drills down into the specifics of your résumé. You must know it inside out to take the greatest advantage of this key portion of your interview. You might be thinking, "Of course, I know what's on my résumé." Don't take it for granted. When major rock groups like The Rolling Stones put together new tours, they have to re-memorize their classic hits — the ones the rest of us know by heart — and practice them all over again. We all forget information that we think of as being a part of ourselves. You must be very clear on *exact* dates, months and years of employment with each company. You must be able to account for and explain any time gaps. Memorize all this information so that you are comfortable with all of your numbers and your accomplishments, how long you remained in each position before you got promoted, why you are looking to leave and what you are looking for in a new position. We call this having a good story to tell. The worst thing you can do is to say something vague like, "I *think* I was there until June of 2001," or "I can't quite remember the month I was promoted, but I *think* it was July of 2002." That doesn't cut it. You will appear unprepared and less sharp than the candidate who says, "Within 12 months, I was promoted to Major Accounts, June 2000. My first year in Major Accounts, I was 135% of quota, ranked #1 out of 12 representatives and promoted 16 months later to National Accounts Manager in October 2001." Like an attorney presenting a case in court, your story must be air tight.

A great interviewee will take pleasure in confidently responding to the question, "Could you walk me through your résumé?" You must be able to do so in a clear, concise and compelling manner and make it the basis of a captivating personal story. You want to pique the interviewer's interest enough to leave them wanting to hear more. One good strategy is to say you will give them the condensed version and expand on any points that are of particular interest.

When you are talking about the accomplishments, you may also pull out your brag book, flipping quickly through the pages and pointing out the relevant documents. This must be practiced and rehearsed as if you were a dancer, actor or athlete going over a tricky play. You need to learn to maintain eye contact with your interviewer as you also point to and turn the pages of the book. Your brag book functions just like the materials used by professionals on a sales call; in this case it is also known as a "site seller." Have your brag book in perfect chronological order so it syncs up with your résumé and you can review it in a timely manner.

However, don't let the brag book distract you from the momentum of the interview. Use it as a tool, but be prepared to disregard it if your interviewer appears disengaged or leads you down another conversational path.

Here is a sample script for summarizing your résumé:

*"After graduating from college, I accepted an offer with Xerox Corporation in outside sales for the downtown Chicago territory. As you may know, Xerox has the number one sales training program in the country, and I was determined to be trained by the best. I had also been advised to learn to sell for one of the top Fortune 500 business products companies if I intended to break into pharmaceutical sales in the future. I started with Xerox in May of 2002 and during my first year in sales, I grew the territory 25%. I was ranked number two out of 25 representatives, completed my first year at 120% of quota and was awarded "rookie of the year." Within 14 months, I was promoted to Major Account Executive to handle all accounts over $1 million in revenue a year. In my second year I went on to accomplish..."* and continue with your professional experience until you come to the present.

When you conclude your professional experience, then you move into the transition into pharmaceutical sales:

*"With 5 years of successful outside sales experience, I am ready to succeed in a career in pharmaceutical sales."*

As you speak, draw parallels between your industry and pharmaceutical sales. Here is a guide to help you draw effective comparisons:

| Business-To-Business Sales Representative | Pharmaceutical Sales Representative |
|---|---|
| 1) Plan sales calls the day before to help maintain maximum efficiency when in the field. | 1) Setup pre-call plan based on territory analysis and prescribing habits. |
| 2) Utilize company sales tools and give sales presentation utilizing "pitch book" to potential customers. | 2) Utilize company sales tools and give sales presentation utilizing "detail piece" to support your pitch. |
| 3) Stay up to date on newest technology on the market and competitive information. | 3) Stay up to date on newest research and clinical data released as well as competitive information. |
| 4) Maintain notes and personal information on clients and buying habits. | 4) Enter daily sales calls into tracking program and evaluate pre- and post-call activity. |

## 3. Behavioral Questions

The smartest interviewers these days rely heavily on what's known as "behavioral interviewing," which studies have proven to be the most effective predictor of who will succeed in a position once they are hired. This means, you will be asked specific questions about how you handled situations similar to those you will encounter in pharmaceutical sales. Often, this method follows the STAR format. This stands for "Situation, Task, Action and Result." It is also known as SAR for "Situation, Action and Result." Over such a line of questioning, an interviewer will sketch out either a general or a specific situation — e.g., handling an angry customer — and ask how, exactly, you have handled such situations in the past. If you've never been asked behavioral interview questions before, keep the STAR acronym in mind. If you do, you'll give the interviewer exactly what he or she is looking for.

### *Answering questions according to the STAR format:*

1. Describe the **Situation** you faced.
2. Give an account of the **Task** you selected to address it.
3. Relate the specific **Actions** you took to complete the task.
4. Report what happened as a **Result**.

The following websites contain more information on STAR and SAR interviewing techniques:

www.quintcareers.com/STAR_interviewing.html
*Features sample behavioral questions*

www.unk.edu/offices/careerserv/students/career_handbook/index.
php?id=2364
*A University of Nebraska website*

# Good Interviewing Preparation Strategies

Be prepared to think on your feet. The behavioral component of the interview resembles an audition. You are, in essence, verbally acting out how you would perform for your prospective employer. Be prepared to offer up specific scenarios from your past. You will probably be asked, for example, to recount specifically the story of how you responded to that irate customer. If you don't have any experience in a particular area, just be honest and say that this is a situation you have yet to encounter. You might ask the interviewer if he or she would like to know how you imagine you might respond.

## TOM'S TIP — SHARPEN YOUR SAW

I HEARD STEPHEN COVEY TELL A STORY ONCE about a man who walks into a forest and sees another man sawing away feverishly at a tree. He notices that the saw is dull and points it out. "That doesn't matter," the man snaps back in response, furiously moving the blade ineffectually against the wood. "I have to cut down this tree!"

GET THE IDEA? Every person knows what to do to sharpen his or her saw. For me, to stay sharp and effective, I do better with at least seven hours a night of sleep and one hour of a cardio workout every day. I also take time to stretch, take yoga classes, lift weights and do core exercises.

WITHOUT ANY OF THESE, I AM SLUGGISH AND MY PATIENCE IS SHORT. I am off my game. I also eat lean foods that are high in protein combined with nuts, fruits and vegetables. I don't eat red meat, and I eat very few dairy products. I balance my work life by spending time out in nature and with my family and friends. I play, find recreation and set aside time for financial research and reading.

IF I DON'T SHARPEN MY SAW, I LOSE MY EFFECTIVENESS. It takes work, but a lot less work than working with a dull instrument.

## CHAPTER ELEVEN

# Interview Questions

**"** Whether you think you can or think you can't, you are right. **"**

**— Henry Ford**

A t some point in your interview, you'll probably want to come "off script." You will have rehearsed. You have memorized a couple of points you want to make. But you should feel comfortable enough to go with the flow of the interview, to respond to any surprises that come your way — and, most important, to speak from the heart. In the words of the utterly unique Dr. Seuss, "Today you are You, that is truer than true. There is no one alive who is Youer than You."

But you'll have better luck being spontaneous *after* you've thoroughly familiarized yourself with the most common questions that come up in the interview setting. You will find many of them in this chapter. Based on my proprietary survey of district managers, here are the Top Ten most frequently asked questions in pharmaceutical sales representative interviews. A district manager for a Fortune 500 company provides some insight as to what he is looking for with each question.

## The Top Ten Most Frequently Asked Questions

1. What are your weaknesses? *This really isn't necessarily about weaknesses. I'm looking for people who are aggressively working on their self-development and can talk about the areas in which they need work. What is their growth plan? Does their reasoning stand up to scrutiny? I am not looking for the need-to-get-better-at-delegation response. I don't like it when candidates dodge this question. Other show stoppers: "I need to learn to close better. I*

*need to become more organized." By the way candidates answer this question; I can tell if they are goal-oriented.*

2. Describe how you worked through a situation with a difficult or dishonest person in your workplace. *Here I'm looking for maturity and sound judgment. This is where someone who is not so mature can slip up. It also gives me a glimpse into their ethics. I'm looking for someone who won't go along with an unethical choice and who won't let the team go along with it either. I'm looking for someone who's going to stand their ground. This is more important than ever for district managers, who have to be very careful about adhering to industry guidelines.*

3. Describe a situation where you had to overcome an obstacle to achieve your goal (the sale). *Here I want to see if this person has a plan in place. I am looking for multi-layers of effort and ideas they thought about before they ran into the obstacle. Were resources brought to bear that are outside of a candidate's sphere of influence?*

4. Why should we hire you? *You've got to be prepared for this question. Here I'm looking for your preparation. Do you have a track record of success? Does a candidate know what makes him or her successful? On the job you're going to get this question every day: "Why should I buy this product?"*

5. Tell me about a time when you faced a challenge — using the STAR format. *I like to ask them to use the STAR format once, and then see if they remember that on the follow-up questions. This shows how good their listening skills are. Often people tend to forget to talk about the result. They'll either downplay the result or take for granted that you know they made the sale. Using the STAR format tells me if you are a good planner. Those with weaker planning and organizational skills tend to have trouble answering this question.*

6. Sell me this.... *I'm looking to see if they do a good job of identifying my needs. Do they link features with benefits? Do they*

*close? How do they close? I'm also looking for comfort level. Are they relaxed? Are their hands shaking? Often I will say, "Go out and learn about a product, and then sell me on it." I'm looking for the initiative they show in finding out about the product. I will ask how they did their research. The ones who go to different sources impress me the most.*

7. Describe your most creative sale and/or your selling style. *Here I want to understand if they are conscious of what their selling style is. If so, chances are that this is someone who has put a lot of attention into continuing to learn. I often follow up this question by asking what books or tapes you've used in your professional development. On the job, I want to know what you are willing to do that your competition is not willing to do. I want to hear about their business plan for a territory. Only a few candidates come in with prepared business plans. Younger candidates need to show a willingness to learn.*

8. Describe a time that you failed and tell me what you learned from it. *If a candidate doesn't respond well, I decide that this is someone who hasn't learned from his or her mistakes. Does he or she take the initiative or have the drive to change? If they're not doing that, I don't want them.*

9. What would you change about your current job or boss, if you could? *If they bash a current boss, that's a big black flag. I'm thinking, "Five years down the line, this guy's going to be making stuff up about me." I'm not looking for sour grapes. I'm looking for constructive comments.*

10. If you were a (symbol, animal, cloud, ice cream flavor) what would you be and why? *I would use this question to see if candidates are quick on their feet. Do the characteristics of the animal or object match up with the characteristics of my "ideal candidate"? How witty are they? Do they have a sense of humor?*

# Other Sample Interview Questions

- What are your biggest strengths?
- What are your current rankings?
- Where are you ranked vs. your peers? Locally, regionally and nationally?
- Do you have performance evaluations? (Refer to your brag book here.)
- Describe a typical day in your current position.
- What is your quota and where are you ranked against your quota?
- What is the most difficult situation you've been put into in your professional career, and how did you handle it?
- What is the toughest sale you've ever made?
- What was the most difficult sale you've lost, and how did you respond?
- How do you handle rejection?
- What are you especially proud of in your career?
- How would your current boss describe you?
- How would one of your current customers describe you?
- Why do your customers buy from you?
- How do you develop rapport with your customers?
- What are the steps in the selling process?
- What do you do to keep improving as a sales person or an individual?
- Why are you looking to leave?
- What do you like most about your current position?
- What do you like least about your current position?
- How do the skill sets of your current position apply to this position?
- What gives you the greatest feeling of achievement in your current position?
- What is your current compensation package?
- What are you looking for in a new compensation package?
- What do you do in your free time? Hobbies?
- What are the last three books/magazines you've read?
- How do you plan and organize your day?
- What constitutes a priority?
- Why did you leave your previous position?
- Why pharmaceutical sales?
- Why do you want to work for our company?

- What do you know about our company?
- What do you know about our industry?
- What type of research have you done?
- Describe a day in the life of a pharmaceutical representative.
- What is the biggest challenge facing a pharmaceutical representative in today's market?
- Are you familiar with managed care?
- Why did you choose your college?
- What was your degree?
- Why did you choose your degree?
- Did you take any science courses, and if so, how did you do? (GPA)?
- What motivates you?
- Who is the best manager you've ever worked for and what made him/her so special?
- What are your career goals and aspirations?
- Are you currently interviewing with any other companies?
- If yes, which ones, and how far along are you?
- What are your short-term and long-term goals?
- Where do you see yourself five years from now?
- What has been the biggest disappointment in your professional career?
- Give me an example of dealing with a difficult co-worker or customer and how you handled it.
- How would you deal with an upset office manager or nurse who is blocking you from seeing a doctor?

**Trick Question:** Just before going to press we learned of a new "gotcha" question being employed in interviews: "Where did you tell your employer you were today?" Companies are using the question to gauge candidates' trustworthiness, and most people slip up in the response. The only correct answer is to say that you took the day as a vacation day.

**For a more thorough list of answers to these questions, go to: www.tomruff.com/candidates/questions.htm**

# Questions for the Interviewer

The following list contains smart and incisive questions for you to pose to your interviewer. Make sure to listen closely to the responses, take notes and ask any natural follow-up questions that occur to you based on the interviewer's responses.

- What are you looking for in a sales representative?
- Who is your number one sales representative, and why?
- Who is your worst sales representative, and why?
- Why is the position open?
- How long has the position been open?
- What shape is the territory currently in?
- What is the territory currently ranked?
- What is the average tenure of a representative on your team?
- How would you describe your management style?
- What does it take to be successful in this position?
- What would it take to make this position the #1 territory in the region and in the country?
- What are some of the challenges a representative would face in this territory?
- What opportunities are there for career advancement and what is it based on?
- What was your background prior to getting into pharmaceutical sales?
- Why did you join this organization?
- What do you like most about working for your company?
- What has kept you here for this long?
- What is the biggest challenge you face as a district manager?
- What is the biggest challenge your sales team faces?
- What are your expectations for your sales team?
- What can your team expect from you as a manager?
- How would you describe your leadership style?
- How would you describe your current sales team?

## CHAPTER TWELVE

# Second, Third and Panel Interviews

" Adversity has the effect of eliciting talents which in prosperous circumstances would have lain dormant. "

**– Horace**

The second and third interviews are just as important as the first. I've seen more candidates than I care to recall treat the third or final interview as if it were a mere "rubber stamp," ease up on their focus and completely blow their chances at the final stage. I want to emphasize that you need to treat each and every person you meet at every stage of the interview process as if he or she knows nothing about you. Never fail to elaborate or lose your intensity in your answers out of a suspicion that your interviewer already knows what you are going to say because you've said it so many times before. If you need to explain, for the 20th time, why you want to go into pharmaceutical sales, do it with as much passion as you did the first time around. In the month before going to press with this book, three of our candidates made it all the way to the final interview, only to be vetoed by the regional manager. So, stay alert. It really is not over until you have a signed offer in hand. Even then, you may need to renegotiate, but more on that in a minute.

Second and third interviews may differ from company to company. Most schedule your first interview with the hiring district manager. While tough, that interview tends to be friendly. The second interview is often with one or even two district managers, sometimes your original interviewer with another you have yet to meet. This allows a second person to offer fresh insights into you as a candidate. Often the second interview is tougher, especially if the hiring district manager is weeding the top choice from a field of contenders. Expect it to last one to three hours, which may include a break. If it is held over breakfast or lunch, choose an entrée that is easy to eat and won't create a mess. Never try to talk or answer questions while your mouth is full.

As mentioned earlier, you will be asked situational questions, such as: "Tell me about a time when you were working on a team, and one person wasn't pulling his weight. What did you do?" Or "Tell me what your friends would say are your strongest qualities and weakest qualities?" Or, "What would your enemies say are your strongest qualities and weakest qualities?" Often, the second district manager will want to see how you act under stress and take a less friendly, more challenging tone. You may also be asked more detailed questions about the products the company sells to check the quality and depth of your research.

My friend Heidi-Anne Mooney, formerly of Abbott, has undergone interviews where she was handed a sales detail piece which she was given five minutes to review before selling it. "They don't expect you to be perfect," she says. "They just want to see if you behave naturally in a sales situation. This is why if you have a friend in the pharmaceutical business, especially one who takes you on a field ride, you should try to practice doing this and ask for tips. Just take an ad out of any magazine and practice selling the product."

Like many of the best sales representatives I've met, Heidi-Anne also practices in front of a mirror and answers questions out loud.

Be prepared to look at both interviewers while you are talking to them. If you can, try to find out from the hiring district manager how many interviewers will be there so you can prepare enough brag books and résumés to hand over once you enter the room. The bottom line is you need to be prepared for the second interview as it will most likely be harder than the first one. For every interview you attend, make sure to get a business card from your interviewer(s) right at the outset of your time together.

The third interview usually means you've passed all the screening, completed the drug test, have a good driving record and your GPA and résumé stats have been cleared. The company is poised to hire you. Your final review is often conducted by your district manager's manager, a regional manager or even a higher-ranking vice-president of sales or marketing. Usually this person has more than 20 years of experience in the industry. You may be required to fly in for a day for this interview, which will run as short as 20 minutes or up to two hours. These interviews may be conducted in private hotel suites, hotel lobbies, coffee shops or even at airports. So, be prepared to contend with a distracting setting.

By this point, you should have done extensive research on the company, know its annual revenue, size, product line, current news accounts of the company and, of course, why you want to work there. The interviewer will ask situational questions, but also may revisit earlier questions about why you want to work in sales, in pharmaceutical sales in particular, for this particular district manager and for this company. You may also be asked if you are willing to relocate. If you can do so, the right answer is always yes.

These interviews may be the least stressful, but never forget that this person has the final say. If he or she doesn't like you or you fail to impress in one way or another, you will be cut.

At the end, write out a thank-you note as soon as possible. The formality and quickness with which you do this may be the deciding factor between you and another candidate. Even if your final interviewer already had a copy of your résumé and brag book, it never hurts to have a fresh copy on hand. All of these preparations show your professionalism and may set you apart from your competition. Knowing that you will have two to three interviews, you want to be sure that you have enough formal suits to wear. Always dress up versus dressing down. If you are interviewing in a hot place like Arizona, still wear your jacket, but feel free to follow the lead of the person interviewing you. If he or she takes off a jacket, go ahead and do the same. However, the more formal your attire, the better.

## Panel Interviews

Often when companies are hiring for multiple positions, they will conduct panel interviews. This allows the managers to assemble in one location and interview numerous candidates at once. Afterwards, they can put their heads together in a brief conference, compare notes and make hiring decisions in much shorter time frames. The great thing about panel interviews is that they allow you to meet several managers at once, and you will learn much more quickly whether you have been successful.

# Keys to a successful panel interview:

1. You must be "on" in the same way you would be for a one-on-one interview. Drink your coffee, do your yoga or go for a walk and get the blood flowing.

2. Prepare for the panel as you would for an interview with one person. However, there is one important difference: be sure to make eye contact with all the different panel members. Establish a routine of answering the question and looking at each interviewer for an equal amount of time as you respond. You do not want to spend most of your time looking at the one person with the largest title. This betrays a lack of consideration for the others. If you slight one or two by ignoring them, they will notice and come away with a poor impression of you.

3. Before the interview starts, ask for business cards from each panel member. This will demonstrate your foresight and ability to take a situation in hand. Also, you won't have to worry about breaking the intensity of your "close" at the interview's end. If you are subtle about it, you may be able to refer to one of the cards during the interview itself, if you momentarily forget a person's name.

4. Close each interviewer and ask each person if they have any concerns or reservations that would prevent them from moving you on to the next step. Use the strategies discussed in Chapter 13.

5. Don't forget to thank them for their time and to assure them that you want the job.

6. Follow up with an email to each individual *that day*. Do not send a group email response. Personalize each email to the individual interviewer (use follow-up from previous). And, as always, make sure to send each person a handwritten thank-you note by regular mail.

A panel interview is not as stressful as it may appear. As long as you have done your research and preparation, you will do a great job.

The best strategy is to bring a blank thank-you note to the interview and — if the district manager is checked into the hotel — write a note that

Dear John Doe,

Thank you for taking the time out of your busy schedule to meet with me Monday afternoon. I believe that we have a good fit based upon my background and the job description.

I am very excited about the prospect of joining ABC company as one of your results oriented sales associates. I look forward to speaking with you again in the next few days. If any additional information will be helpful regarding my candidacy, please do not hesitate to call.

Sincerely,
John Doe

---

you will have delivered to him or her. As soon as you are done, write it out in the lobby or in your car. Personalize it in some way. Do what you can to avoid being generic. Thank the interviewer or interviewers for their time, touch on at least two specific points that were covered in the interview, reiterate your strong desire to work for their company and — once again — close for the job.

Go back in, and give the card to the receptionist at the front desk. You may also tip a bellman to hand-deliver the card to the interviewer in his or her room or conference room.

## Email, voicemail and follow-up:

### 1) Email

In addition to your handwritten note, email affords you the space to expand a little further on why you want the job and why you are the best fit. When you get home, type out an email thanking the interviewer or interviewers for their time, list the top three reasons why you want to work for their company, the top three reasons why they should hire you and close one last time: "I want this job and want to be a part of your team."

## 2) Voicemail

Here, you must use your judgment. If the interview goes exceptionally well and they give you their business cards, you can call the 800-number provided and leave a very *brief* voicemail thanking them for their time and letting them know how excited you are about moving on to the next step. End the voice mails by wishing them a great day. And stop right there. Short, sweet and enthusiastic. Don't ask for or expect a return call.

## 3) Creative Follow-up

As mentioned in the previous chapters, for second and third interviews, you will want to get more creative with your follow-up and put together a packet to send or hand to the interviewer. There are many ways of doing this. If the tone of the interview and the interviewer's personality warrant it, some of our candidates have sent fun, attention-grabbing items like pill-shaped helium balloons with their names on them. If they haven't already used them at an earlier stage of the interview process, many of our candidates follow up by sending any or all of the following items.

A) Top 10 Reasons why you want to work for the company

B) Top 10 Reasons why they should hire you

C) A pill capsule, designed by you, with notes on it "prescribing" yourself, and your unique qualities, for the job

D) Motivational book with a letter inside

E) A business plan

I believe a well-thought-out business plan demonstrates a proactive nature and a thorough understanding of the job. Here is a Power Point plan that was sent by one of our successful candidates.

# ABC Pharmaceuticals

## *Business Transition Plan*
Las Vegas, NV

### Jane Doe
January 15, 2007

# Goals and Objectives

◆ Complete familiarization with ABC products and services, local territories, market and competition

◆ Maintain and expand existing business base in Nevada and Utah

◆ Convert accounts previously lost to competition

◆ Grow volume and market share through new and converted customers and expansion of existing customer business

◆ Continued education and product knowledge

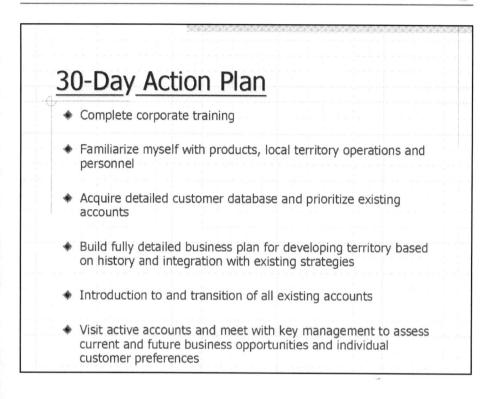

# 30-Day Action Plan

- Complete corporate training

- Familiarize myself with products, local territory operations and personnel

- Acquire detailed customer database and prioritize existing accounts

- Build fully detailed business plan for developing territory based on history and integration with existing strategies

- Introduction to and transition of all existing accounts

- Visit active accounts and meet with key management to assess current and future business opportunities and individual customer preferences

# 60-Day Action Plan

- Familiarize myself with competition

- Integrate, revise and update business plan

- Conduct follow-up visits and communicate effectively with existing customer base

- Visit accounts lost to competition and convert back to ABC products and services

- Continue to update database

- Continue training and education

# 90-Day Action Plan

- ◆ Target accounts to increase existing business
- ◆ Review existing accounts for additional opportunities
- ◆ Build referral system through satisfied customers and field contacts
- ◆ Pursue new business opportunities within hospital communities
- ◆ Continue to conduct follow-up visits and to communicate with existing customer base
- ◆ Re-visit accounts lost to competition that show promise of business recapture
- ◆ Maintain ongoing training and education

# Territory Management

- ◆ Analyze data for all accounts
  - ▪ Prioritize and rank accounts: A, B, C, D
    - ◆ A – Existing high sales or large volume business, pending sales and demos
    - ◆ B – Existing medium sales or medium volume business
    - ◆ C – Small or zero volume with potential for more business
    - ◆ D – No immediate potential for business
  - ▪ Products and supplies used
    - ◆ Studies and materials given by corporate
    - ◆ Internet research
  - ▪ Map geographic locations
    - ◆ Group accounts and calls

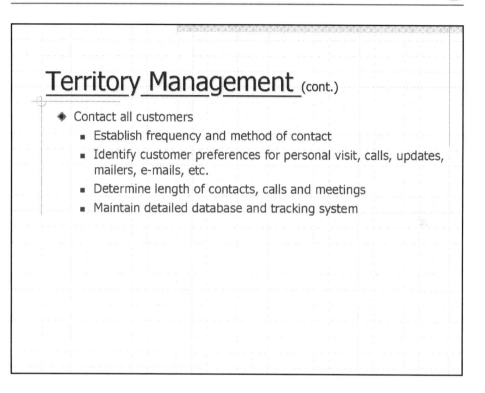

# Territory Management (cont.)

- Contact all customers
  - Establish frequency and method of contact
  - Identify customer preferences for personal visit, calls, updates, mailers, e-mails, etc.
  - Determine length of contacts, calls and meetings
  - Maintain detailed database and tracking system

# Resource Requirements

- Corporate management guidance, training and familiarization with ABC practices and preferences

- Marketing and sales management guidance in transitioning of accounts and development of ongoing territory strategy

- Availability of management and technical personnel support to enhance account development

- Initial and continuing education and training

*A final note:* Once you have gone through all your interviews, you are still not done. Before offering you a position, pharmaceutical companies will complete the process of running a thorough background check. In addition to checking your driving record and administering a drug test, your potential employer will also run a credit check and see if you have a criminal record. If you anticipate a problem in any of these areas, take the initiative and raise the matter beforehand.

## CHAPTER THIRTEEN

# The Close

66 Everything that is worthwhile in life is scary. . . .
If it is not fearful, it is not worthwhile. 99

**– Paul Tornier**

U p to this point, I've told you that the most critical part of the interview is the research and preparation you do beforehand. But all of that is null and void if you ignore or gloss over *The Close*. I can't say this strongly enough: **you must close!** You can do an amazing job preparing for the interview, show up brimming with enthusiasm in an immaculate suit and nail every question, but if you don't close well, you are finished. Kaput. Your ability to close is the acid test of your ability to sell your product. We've had clients who sang our candidates' praises, but refuse to bring them back for an interview because of this mistake. "She didn't close me," they tell us. To us, those words are fingernails on a black board. It's like presenting flowers to your spouse and forgetting to say, "Happy Anniversary." They might end up in the trash.

This isn't caprice on the part of the companies. They simply know that without this skill you won't be selling any of their products to their customers. You're all show and no substance. As a good friend, who is a district manager at one of the largest pharmaceutical companies, puts it, "I like to be closed hard. I don't like them beating around the bush. I want them to ask me for the job."

Good advice. And, yet, you have to earn your close. If you were to close my friend too hard early in the process, or without having sufficiently made your case, the strategy would backfire on you.

Here's a good way to start your close. You can use this in any of your interviews: one-on-one, on the phone or in front of a panel.

# Sample Closing Script

"After meeting with me and reviewing my résumé, do you have **any** reservations or concerns that would prevent you from bringing me back for another interview?"

Wait here for a moment for a response. If they do have reservations, you can address them now. For example, an interviewer might say, "I'm concerned that you don't have enough business-to-business sales experience." By this time, you should be deeply familiar with any potential weaknesses on your résumé. You should have anticipated questions of this sort and practiced — role-played — responding to them. Here you might say, "I understand your concern about my lack of business-to-business experience" — it's always a good idea to repeat back their concern to demonstrate that you do indeed understand it and are able to listen attentively to criticism — "… however, I feel that my strong sales record with my current employer makes up for it. Furthermore, as I hope I've demonstrated, I have a tremendous desire and capacity to learn and grow." If there is more that you can add, do so.

Once you've finished, ask if this response has fully addressed the concern. If not, ask for them to elaborate on their considerations, and then respond to those as well. Do this until you are reasonably certain they are comfortable with your explanations. Then ask them if there are any other concerns they might have. This may sound like a laborious process, but it is very valuable. Believe me, anything you leave unaddressed will certainly come up as the district manager discusses your candidacy after you've left. Your ability to fully address perceived weaknesses will speak volumes in your favor.

My high-ranking district manager friend is most impressed by "multi-level" closes. "After reiterating your strongest attributes," he says, "you might first ask, 'When could I meet with your regional manager?' The next thing should be, 'Can you give me a commitment right here for my interview?' If someone has closed me well, I will go ahead and commit to it." However, this is a delicate dance. If you sense resistance on the part of your interviewer, back off. You don't want to come off like a used-car salesman. "Earning the right to close indicates someone who has done his homework," my friend explains. "They need to be tuned in to my body language and the answers I'm giving them. They know they've nailed the answers. You're not going to go in and, at forty minutes, ask for the job. If it's a good interview, we've been together for an hour and a half. Then they've earned the right to close me."

Once you have earned that right, we come to the fun part of the close.

## Part Two of the Close

This is where you dig deep down in your heart and soul and speak from a place of sincerity, intensity and single-minded purpose. You take control of the close by addressing your interviewer or interviewers by name, then pause for a full three seconds — this may feel odd, but do it; you are creating a lasting impression — to make sure you have their undivided attention. Using their names will get them to stop any fidgeting. Go right to the edge of what feels like an uncomfortable silence and stare right into your interviewer(s')'s eyes. Then confidently say your own version of the following.

> "Before I leave here today, I want you to know that *I want this job*. (pause) I want to be a part of your team for these reasons… (give them your top three reasons). I would be the best fit for the position because … (give them the top three reasons). What do I need to do at this point to come and work for you?" For an even more direct approach, you might simply say, "What do I need to do to get this job?" Then — and this is very important — **say absolutely nothing**. Nothing at all! Even if you feel uncomfortable, remain silent.

As tempting as it might be to talk when there is dead silence, don't. Wait for them to respond. This is a great chance to demonstrate your composure at a critical moment. This is a great way to close. As I've already explained, sales managers want closers. They need them. Even if you feel uncomfortable, close the interview anyway. Closing is all about taking charge of your life. If you haven't done so before, there's no better time to start than right now!

Pharmaceutical companies are looking for seasoned professionals. They are not in the business of providing basic sales instruction on their own. They are planning to dive right in and invest more than $100,000 to teach you about the science behind their products, the disease states those products address and the necessary ins and outs of the ever-changing medical world. They need somebody who is ready for this sort of advanced training. With a strong close, you demonstrate that you are worth their investment.

Before or after your final close, you may find it appropriate to ask some or all of the following closing questions:

## Closing Questions for Interviewer

- How many people have you interviewed for this position?
- Where do I rank versus the other candidates?
- Is there anything else you or I need to know before I leave?
- What is the next step?
- Can we confirm a second interview? (This is a judgment call)
- (If they won't commit) When can I expect to hear from you?
- May I follow up via email?

Always make sure you have a business card. Thank them and shake their hands, with a smile.

## TOM'S TIP — YOUR PERSONAL CONSTITUTION

BACK IN THE EARLY '90S, I wrote out my own Personal Constitution. It's a list of principles that I strive to live by each and every day. Especially when faced with a dilemma, I look at this list and it helps steer me in the right direction.

RIGHT UP TOP, I've got my commitment to my health, including specific food, sleep and exercise guidelines. Another principle is to live by the Golden Rule. Rather than react if a person is unkind or unhelpful, I try to stop and consider things from his or her perspective. This helps eliminate conflict in my life.

THIS CONSTITUTION IS A LIVING DOCUMENT. It doesn't sit in a drawer. I've got it with me on my TREO and in my journal. Pretty much every decision I make every day gets filtered through these principles. I've changed it periodically through the years, but not in the past year and a half.

I CREDIT MY PERSONAL CONSTITUTION with helping me stick with my core values, come what may.

# CHAPTER FOURTEEN

## The Offer Stage

**❝ I will prepare and someday my chance will come. ❞**

**— Abraham Lincoln**

The offer stage often requires diplomacy. There are four main component parts to consider.

1. Receiving an offer
2. Negotiating salary
3. Resigning
4. Beware counteroffers

## Receiving an offer

If you receive an offer from a company, CONGRATULATIONS! Even if you are not sure if you are going to accept, or if you want to try to negotiate more money before you do, you need to stop and acknowledge the great job you did to secure an offer with a pharmaceutical company. In a competitive field, you've distinguished yourself from the crowd.

You've got two options at this point:

1) If the offer is the same as what you had discussed with the interviewer and you are prepared to accept, do so on the spot. Say "Thank you" and express how excited you are about the opportunity. You are ready to get to work and you want to become the number one sales representative in their company. Ask for the offer in writing so you can make sure everything in writing is consistent with the verbal offer. If all of the details are the same as you had discussed, sign the offer and give it back to them.

# Negotiating Salary

2) If the offer is lower than what you had expected, or if there are some terms you would like to negotiate, continue to display enthusiasm for the job. Presume that you will work your differences out. If that presumption is correct, you don't want to leave an impression that you were a complainer or had a bad attitude. Tell the interviewer you are honored by the offer and express your gratitude for his or her time and consideration. Then, mention that you have a few remaining questions.

The main thing to remember when trying to negotiate more money is to present all the reasons you are worth it, in the same way an attorney presents evidence in a court of law. You want to make the reasons crystal clear to motivate an interviewer to go back to her boss and use your very same line of reasoning. Arm your interviewer with the necessary information. And don't let your pride keep you from taking a great position if you didn't get everything you asked for. I've seen candidates walk away from wonderful jobs over a mere $2,000. Break that down and you're not pursuing your dream job over just $38.50 a week.

In large measure, your success depends on how you present your case. Remain positive, excited, appreciative, optimistic and confident that you will resolve your differences.

Here's one potential script:

## Sample renegotiation script

> "Based on my research into industry standards, including my knowledge of the other companies with which I have been interviewing, a base salary of $48,000 is low. I have five years of successful outside sales experience, I'm already making $50,000 on my existing base salary and I would like to have an increase in my pay. Do you have any flexibility on the compensation package?" And, then, *say absolutely nothing!*

You may be in for an awkward silence but, no matter what, do *not* crack! Wait for a response. Typically, the interviewer will say she needs to discuss the matter with her boss. Or she will simply tell you no. Either way, you need to be prepared to keep your poise.

# Resigning

Meet with your boss in person to resign. This is the most professional way to go. However, if schedules don't permit and you must resign in a timely manner, schedule a phone conversation and submit a two-week notice. Let him or her know you will fax a signed letter of resignation, as well as mail a hard copy.

Remember that your current position paved the way for you to break into pharmaceutical sales. Always be respectful and, remember, never burn bridges. Your paths may indeed cross again, so leave as gracefully as you can. You are a professional and all of your actions — and inactions — will accumulate as your career progresses. You want to develop a reputation as a person of character and integrity.

# Beware Counteroffers

According to a variety of studies, more than half of those candidates who accept counteroffers are gone after six months to a year. In most cases, I advise candidates against taking them. If you are presented with one, consider the following:

1. Reconsider all the reasons you were looking to leave in the first place. Money is usually only one of them and, quite probably, not the driving one. According to a 2001 study that examined approximately 20,000 exit interviews, the number one reason people leave jobs is "poor supervisory behavior." If this is one of your complaints, the bump in compensation won't make a difference.
2. If you decide to stay, your boss will know that — behind his or her back — you were job hunting. Your loyalty will forever more be called into question. Subconsciously, you will be considered a risk especially when the prospect of promoting you over other workers arises.
3. Often employers will only hang onto you long enough to replace you. Machiavellian, but true.

Don't make the mistake of letting some extra money supplant legitimate reasons why you were unhappy in the first place. The thrill of the higher salary will soon wear off and you'll find yourself back where you started. You'll always ask yourself why your boss didn't pay you more on his own first, rather than waiting until you forced his hand.

# Letter of Resignation

Technically, a letter of resignation is not required, but it does provide a legal document of your departure and is a professional courtesy to your current employer.

Write one that is concise and to-the-point. Do not address specifics about your new job, but make your resignation formal by putting it down on paper, giving a two-week notice. Thank your current employer for the experience you have received and express your appreciation for everything the company has done for you. Close it respectfully.

## Sample Letter of Resignation

Date_____

Dear_____,

This will serve as my official letter of resignation from (your company) effective today, (today's date). I will honor my full two-week notice unless instructed otherwise.

I would like to thank you for a wonderful experience and let you know how much I value our professional relationship as well as my relationships with my co-workers. I have learned a great deal from everyone I worked with at (your company). I will carry those lessons with me throughout my future career and my life.

I will do everything I can to make this a smooth, professional and seamless transition. Please let me know how this can best be accomplished during my final two weeks.

Respectfully,
Your Name

## CHAPTER FIFTEEN

# How They Did It

*The Tom Ruff survey of 20 district managers
and 150 sales representatives*

# DISTRICT MANAGERS

**1.** How often do you meet with your sales representatives?

| | |
|---|---|
| Quarterly | 35.3% |
| Monthly | 35.2% |
| Biweekly | 11.8% |
| Weekly | 5.9% |
| Several times a week | 5.9% |
| Daily | 5.9% |

**2.** How often do you talk to your sales representatives on the phone?

| | |
|---|---|
| Daily | 47.1% |
| 3-4 times a week | 23.5% |
| Weekly | 29.4% |

**3.** Is your company planning on hiring in the next 3-6 months?

| | |
|---|---|
| Yes | 93.8% |
| No | 6.2% |

**4.** Do you anticipate any sales force expansions within your organization within the next year?

| | |
|---|---|
| Yes | 70.6% |
| No | 29.4% |

**5.** Do you have any new products that you're expecting to launch within the next year?

| | |
|---|---|
| Yes | 76.5% |
| No | 23.5% |

**6.** What is an ideal background for pharmaceutical sales representatives?

| | |
|---|---|
| Business-to-business sales (e.g.: copier, payroll, long distance, business forms) | 43.8% |
| Previous pharmaceutical sales | 37.4% |
| Clinical (e.g.: nurse, lab tech, physician's assistant) | 18.8% |

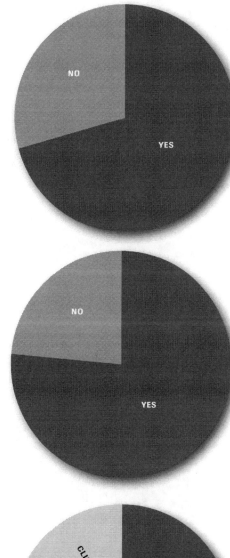

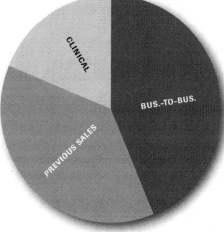

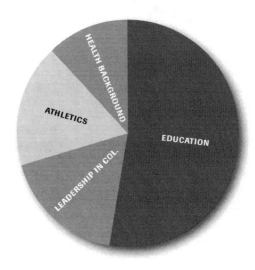

**7.** Of the following possible backgrounds for job candidates, which is most important?

| | |
|---|---|
| Education (e.g., science background) | 53.0% |
| Leadership in college | 17.6% |
| College or professional athletics | 17.6% |
| Healthcare background (nurse, physician's assistant, etc.) | 11.8% |

**8.** What is the best way for a candidate without any outside sales experience to break into the industry?

**SAMPLE RESPONSES:**

- To work with the part-time pharmaceutical representative organizations or to gain sales experience in a similar healthcare organization.

- Personally, I think all people should gain some kind of formal sales training, prior to pharma sales, preferably with a Fortune 500 company. However, if I had to give advice to someone without outside sales experience, I would say research the industry, the companies (go way beyond the company website), the competitors and even the disease states prior to the interviews. Find someone to take you out into the field more than once to make sure, 1) you actually understand (at least on surface) what the job entails, and 2) to demonstrate initiative, creativity and drive.

- Sell copiers for two years.

- Hire a recruiter! A candidate needs to demonstrate the ability to communicate effectively with people. Toastmasters, teaching, an outgoing personality, interviewing strongly. . . . It all helps.

- Network with other representatives in the area as well as visit local offices to understand what this industry is all about.

- Working with recruiters.

- Know someone.

- This would be tough. . . . You should meet as many different people in the industry as you can, conduct field travel and have a full understanding of our day-to-day job and expectations. Furthermore, you will need to demonstrate that other things you have done "carry over" similar skill sets that are needed in pharma sales.

- Learn the medicine behind the product.

- Start to work at another sales job for 12 months prior to trying to get into the industry.

**9.** How important is GPA to you and
your company?

| | |
|---|---|
| 10 (Extremely Important) | 31.3% |
| 9 | 12.4% |
| 8 | 6.3% |
| 7 | 31.3% |
| 6 | 12.4% |
| 1 (Not Important) | 6.3% |

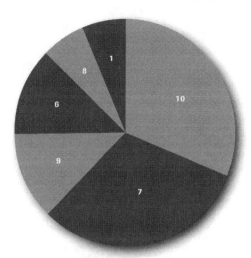

**10.** What is your minimum GPA
requirement?

| | |
|---|---|
| None | 43.8% |
| 2.5 | 6.2% |
| 3.0 | 37.5% |
| 3.5 and above | 12.5% |

**11.** Do you read cover letters?

| | |
|---|---|
| Yes | 38.2% |
| No | 61.8% |

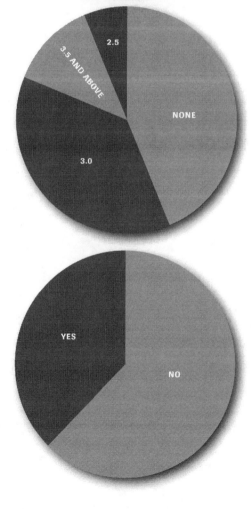

**12.** What do you look for when reviewing a résumé?

**SAMPLE ANSWERS:**

- Brevity, sales experiences, gaps in work experiences, creative programs or successes that are listed with explanation.

- Strong business-to-business sales with quantifiable results. Diverse experiences. Leadership skills and projects. Straightforward language, bullet-pointed and easy to read. Get to the point: why would I want to hire you and what have you done that would best fit you for a very competitive industry?

- Numbers and leadership.

- Candidates who have the whole package: degree, outside sales success, two jobs out of college, progression within their current company, extra-curricular activities with a competitive nature.

- University degree, GPA, experience, years within a position.

- 1. Years of experience with each company 2. Successful track record 3. Awards.

- Examples of leadership.

- Sales experience, college leadership, GPA and no gaps. Also sufficient time at each job.

- Achievement and work ethic.

**13.** Where do you find the majority of the candidates that you hire?

| | |
|---|---|
| Recruiter | 43.8% |
| Job boards: Monster, Hotjobs, etc. | 31.3% |
| Employee referral | 25.0% |
| Human Resources | 6.3% |
| Personal referral | 6.3% |

Note: total exceeds 100%

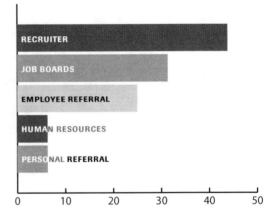

**14.** What are the top three attributes you look for when interviewing a candidate?

| | |
|---|---|
| Experience | 62.5% |
| Personality | 56.3% |
| Communication skills | 56.3% |
| Clinical/science background | 25.0% |
| Professional image | 6.3% |
| Sense of humor | 6.3% |

Note: total exceeds 100%

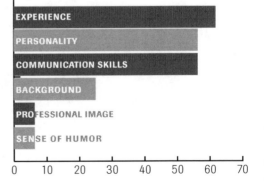

**15.** What is the biggest mistake a candidate can make in an interview?

**SAMPLE ANSWERS:**

- Frequently, I interview healthcare professionals who, during the interview, confide that they really want to work in corporate or in research positions.

- I have interviewed people who did not know anything beyond the name of the company and products they were potentially going to sell. If I see that they have not researched the company, company products and don't have at least a top-line understanding of the disease states, they are out of the running for me. Experienced in the industry or not, they are out.

- DUI.

- Not closing me.

- Not being prepared. A candidate must research the company, the drugs and the competitors. Have questions prepared ahead of time for the interviewer.

- Talking negatively about the company that he or she is working for.

- Telling me they need the job to pay off credit card debt — it has happened!

- Overly confident, ill-prepared, without an understanding of the job. No documentation of their past results.

- Exhibiting a lack of professionalism.

- Negative/sarcastic attitude.

---

**16.** What is the best advice you would give someone regarding interview preparation?

**SAMPLE ANSWERS:**

- Talk to someone in the position and preferably within the district to determine the needs of the district manager, the company and the issues within the company and the open territory. Prepare and research the company and the position thoroughly using the Internet, by interviewing current representatives and competing representatives.

- Step one: company website. Step two: Google the company, products and disease states. Print everything that will be useful in the interview. Read, highlight, gain a broad understanding of the company from company-provided and external sources (bring information to the interview). Spend time in the field, talk to pharmacists, medical doctors and/or people in the industry. Find out about your interviewer, if possible. Google his or her name and see if anything comes up (colleges, interests, etc.). You may not need all this information, but it can help in your interview. Develop an interview "platform" — what are the 5 Core Reasons why you are the candidate for the job. Obviously this should be built on the absolute strengths you possess.

- Practice.

- Learn everything you can about my company prior to coming to meeting me. Never come without knowing about my products and my industry if you do not have experience in the field.

- Have a "brag book" ready and know how to use it. Many candidates bring a hardcopy with them and then hand it to me at the end for my "review." Instead, they need to use the brag book like a sales aid, to help demonstrate their successes and to sell themselves.

- Need a professionally done résumé (short, concise and honest). Be on time.

- Be yourself. Prepare for the company and interviewer.

- Know the job, drugs and territory as well as you can prior to meeting with the manager. Come prepared with an action plan that shows the manager what you would do if you had the job!

- Learn the products.

- Talk to someone in the industry.

**17.** What is the best advice you would give someone for the interview itself?

**SAMPLE ANSWERS:**

- Have a professional appearance. Make eye contact. Ask thorough and thoughtful questions regarding the position.
- Be polished, both verbally and physically. (Shine those shoes.) Make sure your responses answer the question. Speak clearly, be precise and succinct.
- Be yourself.
- Good eye contact and handshake at the beginning, intelligent questions that you could not have gotten answers to off of our website. SELL ME.
- Be yourself. A manager wants to first feel comfortable with a candidate. At the end, I always ask myself, could I spend two days in a car with this person?
- 1. Showcase your success on the résumé and during the interview 2. Be honest.
- Follow Tom's advice.
- Be honest.

**18.** Are there any factors that automatically eliminate a candidate during the interview?

- Inappropriate clothing or appearance (e.g., 2+ inch nails), poor eye contact, lack of preparation and broken English or lack of a command of English.
- Lying, tardiness (failing to call if you are running late), dressing unprofessionally and failing to prepare or research. Those are my automatics.
- DUI.
- Dirty fingernails, cursing, using inappropriate slang, not closing me at the end.
- Lack of communication skills. Low GPA. Lack of passion.
- 1. DUI 2. Lack of a college degree 3. Lack of driver's license 4. Too much enthusiasm.
- Lack of conversation skills. Being confrontational or defensive about your work/college experience/GPA. First impressions are everything. This is what will matter with our customers.
- Unprofessional dress.
- Lack of preparation, being late to the interview or inappropriate dress.

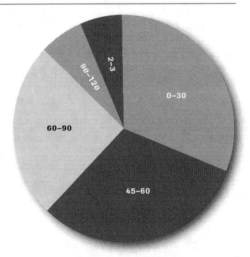

**19.** How long is a typical interview?

| | |
|---|---|
| 0–30 minutes | 31.3% |
| 45–60 minutes | 31.3% |
| 60–90 minutes | 24.8% |
| 90–120 minutes | 6.3% |
| 2–3 hours | 6.3% |

**20.** How many steps are in your interview process?

| | |
|---|---|
| 1 | 35.3% |
| 5 | 35.3% |
| 4 | 23.5% |
| 3 | 5.9% |

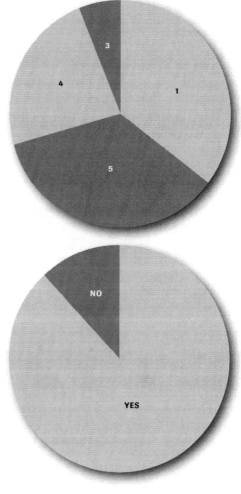

**21.** Do you like to see a brag book from a candidate?

| | |
|---|---|
| Yes | 88.2% |
| No | 11.8% |

**22.** Any tips on what makes a successful brag book?

**SAMPLE ANSWERS:**

• Sales results, awards, projects.

• Lots of numbers.

• Solid documentation for sales achievements.

• Anything that demonstrates what your résumé states: sales numbers, projects, awards, recommendations.

• Short and concise. Performance reviews. Letters of recommendations from previous managers or the company. Awards that you have won. Bio of your experience.

• Include sales results, field contact reports, annual reviews, awards.

• Concise current examples. Knowing what's in it.

• RESULTS!!!!!

• Achievement, not bullshit.

**23.** Describe your top representatives. What do they do differently from the rest of the team?

**SAMPLE ANSWERS:**

- The top representative knows his or her accounts thoroughly and sells accounts proactively. He is a team player and is willing to help all in the district, working smartly and with exceptional focus on business opportunities and the appropriate ROI.

- They take the initiative. They are proactive. The best representatives stay on top of current materials, reprints and current medical trends. Good MD planning and strategic planning is key. They proactively help develop other representatives and also bring value to the offices they visit.

- Planning.

- Passionately pursues the business and knows that every contact is valuable, never missing an opportunity to make the most of each one.

- Top representatives have a personal drive to succeed in all they do. They strive to have the best product knowledge, detailed business acumen and strong customer relationships. They view each call as important, with the potential to bring them one step closer to the top of the company rankings.

- Excellent business sense. Long-term thinker. Excellent computer skills. Excellent sales skills. Excellent product knowledge. Excellent multitasker.

- They are consistent with their performance, meeting or exceeding quota, maintaining product knowledge. They have strong selling skills, and administrative talents.

- Great planning and organization.

- They work harder and are team players.

**24.** Describe your worst representative. What do they do differently from the rest of the team?

**SAMPLE ANSWERS:**

- They are unable to focus their territory and see all the accounts as equal. They are reactive. They tend to be more victim rather than the victor. They are very poor time and administrative managers.

- Makes eight calls a day and goes home. No planning, no initiative. They lack passion and a sense of purpose. That is obvious. But sometimes the worst representative is the representative who cannot look inward and make necessary changes to improve himself and his performance. Blaming external factors rather than adjusting to change is always a bad sign.

- Planning.

- Makes the mistake of not closing every time. Not aggressive enough.

- I believe bad representatives have found themselves in the wrong industry for the wrong reasons. I believe when people do not work (the "10 to 2ers"), they are over their head. They usually do not have strong product knowledge, so they are afraid to talk to customers. They are afraid of questions physicians may have for them that they do not have answers for. That is usually the start to a downward trend of making fewer and fewer sales calls, until they are out of a job. Worse than the representative without product knowledge, is the representative who is satisfied with just doing the minimum, without product-messaging and closes. This representative does not find she is part of the team for very long. It usually takes managers very little time to assess whether or not a representative is truly working.

- Bad planning and organization. Average selling skills. Average product knowledge. Average computer skills. Short-term thinker. Average business acumen.

- Poor selling skills and product knowledge. Not calling on the right physicians with the right frequency and message.

- Non-responders to inquiries. Late on paperwork, requests from district manager and team.

- Selfish.

**25.** What is the most rewarding part of being in the pharmaceutical industry?

**SAMPLE ANSWERS:**

• The ability to make a difference in a patient's life and to enhance the quality of their lives through your specific products.

• People live longer today because of the part we play in the field of medicine. Even if the medical doctor prescribes a competitor (though I would prefer it to be mine), the conversations we have with medical doctors may push them to treat more aggressively in a disease state and, in the end, people will have a better quality of life. As a manager, developing people and creating an environment where people can professionally enhance their lives, is an awesome responsibility. Pharmaceutical representatives (the good ones) are some of the hardest working individuals in the selling industry. To get in the industry is not the hardest part of pharma sales (as some people think), but being excellent and bringing value to the customer actually is the hardest part. But, once achieved, it can become one of the most rewarding career paths.

• Self-satisfaction.

• Flexibility, lifestyle, ability to create my own destiny.

• This is truly the best job for long-term growth. Pharma companies hire people for long-term development, for the leadership they can bring to the organization. People can develop themselves both professionally and personally in this industry. We learn about sales, business development, products, management and how to influence people. And we have fun doing it.

• Being able to help patients and caregivers with their health and quality of life.

**26.** What is your annual income?

| | |
|---|---|
| $75,000-100,000 | 11.1% |
| $100,000-150,000 | 33.3% |
| More than $150,000 | 55.6% |

$75,000-100,000

$100,000-150,000

MORE THAN $150,000

0    10    20    30    40    50    60

# SALES REPRESENTATIVES

**1.** How did you get your job in pharmaceutical sales?
(Check all that apply.)

| | |
|---|---|
| Recruiter | 49% |
| Personal referral | 25.2% |
| Networking | 18.5% |
| Pharmaceutical sales representative referral | 15.2% |
| Job Board (e.g.: Monster, Hotjobs, Medzilla) | 13.2% |
| Company website job postings | 8.6% |
| Job fair | 9.3% |
| Newspaper | 3.3% |

Note: total exceeds 100%

**2.** Approximately how many interviews did you go through with your current company before you received an offer?

| | |
|---|---|
| 1–2 | 30.4% |
| 3 | 34.5% |
| 4 | 21.6% |
| 5 | 8.8% |
| More than 5 | 4.7% |

**3.** How long did the entire interview process take, from the time you started interviewing for a pharmaceutical sales job until the time you accepted your current position, in weeks or months?

| | |
|---|---|
| 1-2 weeks | 13.2% |
| 3-4 weeks | 27.8% |
| 1-2 months | 28.5% |
| 3-4 months | 11.9% |
| 5-6 months | 9.9% |
| 6-9 months | 4% |
| 10-12 months | 0.7% |
| 12-18 months | 3.3% |
| More than 5 years | 0.7% |

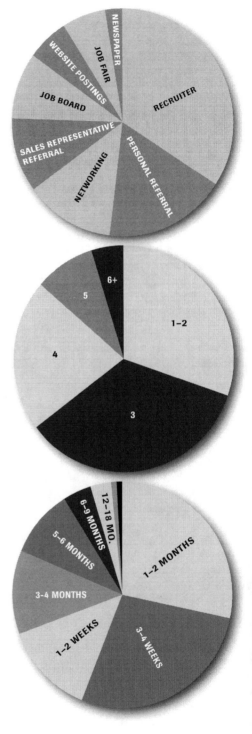

**4.** If you did not previously work in pharmaceutical sales, what was your background?

| | |
|---|---|
| Business-to-business sales (e.g.: copier, payroll, long distance, business forms) | 39.3% |
| Medical sales | 24.7% |
| Other | 21.3% |
| Entry level (no sales experience or recent college graduate) | 9.1% |
| Clinical (e.g.: nurse, lab tech, physician's assistant) | 5.6% |

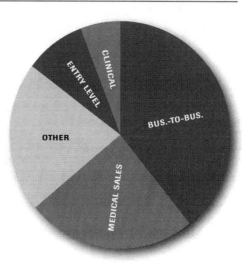

**5.** What were the most important factors in landing your job in pharmaceutical sales? (Choose up to three.)

| | |
|---|---|
| Previous sales experience | 67.3% |
| Personality/sense of humor | 57.3% |
| Professional image and presentation | 55.3% |
| Education | 34.0% |
| Leadership experience | 30.7% |
| Brag book | 24.0% |
| Healthcare background | 12.7% |
| Athletic experience | 8.0% |

Note: Total exceeds 100%

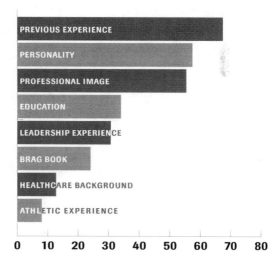

**6.** What was the BEST resource for researching companies while interviewing?

| | |
|---|---|
| Internet | 50.0% |
| Networking | 24.0% |
| Company websites | 21.3% |
| Library | 2.7% |
| Trade magazines | 1.3% |
| Newspapers | 0.7% |

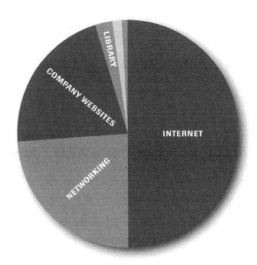

**7.** How would you rate your overall satisfaction with your career in pharmaceutical sales?

| | |
|---|---|
| 10 (Ecstatic) | 6.0% |
| 9 | 18.1% |
| 8 | 33.6% |
| 7 | 22.8% |
| 6 | 5.4% |
| 5 | 3.4% |
| 4 | 4.0% |
| 3 | 2.7% |
| 2 | 2.0% |
| 1 (Miserable) | 2.0% |

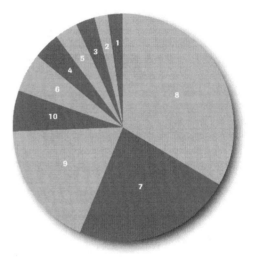

## CHAPTER SIXTEEN

# Working With Recruiters

**"** Be bold and mighty forces will come to your aid. **"**

— Basil King

It is important to understand the best way to work successfully with a recruiter so you can make it an enjoyable, win-win experience. First off, in contacting a recruiter, remember that you will not be the first call of the day. A good recruiter will receive more than a hundred phone calls and more than a hundred emails daily.

One of our biggest pet peeves is when a job candidate calls and launches into a monologue about her tremendous résumé — without determining whether or not my colleagues or I have time to speak. We may have two other candidates on hold and a third sitting before us. Always ask, right off the bat, if this is a good time to talk. The simple act of inquiring increases your chances that it will be. It behooves you to have the recruiter's full, undivided attention. If it is not a good time, say that you would be happy to call later. You can also speed up the process by asking if he or she would prefer that you email your résumé prior to your conversation. When you call a recruiter, let the recruiter know who referred you, especially if the referral came from a pharmaceutical sales representative.

Before even picking up the phone, however, be prepared. Have a copy of your résumé in front of you. If the person who answers is free to talk, tell him or her about the research you've already conducted into the pharmaceutical industry. Let the recruiter know you are serious about your job search and will do everything in your power to land a job in the industry. If you do, they will return your resolve with their own.

If at all possible, go the extra mile to come and visit your recruiter in person. This is something we ask of our candidates whenever possible.

It can be the key difference in motivating a recruiter to get behind your cause.

## Questions for the Recruiter

- Do you specialize in placing pharmaceutical sales representatives?
- What is the ideal background you are looking for in a candidate?
- After reviewing my résumé and discussing my background, do you feel comfortable representing me?
- What are the challenges you think we will face if we work together?
- What is your preferred mode of communication? Email or phone?
- Will you contact me before presenting or sending my résumé out to a client? (This is especially important if you work in the industry)
- Would you like me to call you after the interview to debrief?
- What is the best way for me to stay in touch with you regarding checking my status for potential interviews? How often?
- Do you have any exclusive relationships with companies in the pharmaceutical industry?

If you follow these guidelines, you will greatly increase your chances of working successfully with a recruiter:

- Be careful and selective about choosing recruiters to whom you will send your résumé.
- Meet face-to-face.
- Ask the recruiter to secure permission from you before presenting your résumé to any company.
- Ask for advice about each person you are interviewing with.
- Follow the recruiter's advice about preparing for an interview. Do what he or she says to do.
- Let the recruiter see your brag book and suggest ways to improve it.
- Follow up with the recruiter after each interview.
- Do what you say you are going to do.

# CHAPTER SEVENTEEN

## Voices

**"** It's time to start living the life you've imagined. **"**

— Henry James

*Representatives describe how they broke in and explain why they love doing what they do.*

There are so many ways to break in. As part of my survey, I asked respondents to tell me stories about the successful strategies candidates employed to get their jobs. Despite my 18 years in the industry, even I was surprised by the results.

- One candidate stood in front of his local hospital on a hot day handing out bottles of water to sweaty sales representatives. He'd stuck his résumé, like a label, onto each one.
- Another man washed the car of a pharmaceutical company district manager regularly until he was granted an interview (although it worked for him, we don't advise this approach; you don't want to be mistaken for a "squeegee guy" or a stalker!).
- One military man conducted his job hunt via phone and email while he was stationed in Iraq. He got the job without a face-to-face interview and met his new district manager six days after his tour ended.
- Some of our candidates have printed up RX prescription pads with their interviewers' names on them and their own names listed as the only acceptable cure.
- Others send a pill bottle with a label containing the same information.
- One woman we know sent a district manager a shoe with a note inside that read, "Just trying to get my foot in the door."
- Another woman took a different tack when asked whom she most admired. Instead of Albert Einstein or Helen Keller, she chose

Crocodile Dundee. Her explanation: "He takes a lot of risks. He is an expert in his field. He LOVES what he does. And he is paid well for doing it."

- One exceptionally proactive individual spent a month eating lunch at a hospital cafeteria dressed up like a question mark (we kid you not). By the end of that time, he'd drawn so many doctors into conversations that he figured out which medicines *he* wanted to sell. He applied to pharmaceutical companies that sold those drugs and got a job by including letters from his new doctor-lunch companions explaining why they would buy from him. I couldn't have dreamed up that strategy.

The following are short histories of how different individuals broke in by using more conventional means to overcome a variety of challenges.

## Putting a positive spin on a low GPA

John Clayton began his college years at Purdue taking pre-med classes, only to find that he wasn't cut out for the long years in school required to practice medicine like his father. Instead he majored in animal science so that, if need be, he could fall back on a career managing the family farm that he and his father owned on the side. However, John pinned his hopes on pharmaceutical sales as the next-best career in the medical field.

To prepare himself to interview with pharmaceutical companies, John took advantage of opportunities on his college campus. When companies like Cargill and ADM started interviewing students, he jumped at the chance to polish his interviewing skills, though he had no intention of working for either outfit.

By the time he'd gotten several interviews under his belt, he was ready to begin his job search in the pharmaceutical industry. Networking wasn't a problem. He printed up 50 copies of his résumé and drafted his father into the effort. When pharmaceutical representatives came to his office, John's dad would listen for five or ten minutes on the condition that the representative forward John's résumé on to their district managers or to other companies who were hiring. To thank his dad, John would buy lunch for everyone who worked in his father's office.

In this way, John was able to secure eight or nine interviews.

During each, he was prepared to answer the GPA question. "When they would say, 'You don't have a 4.0 or a 3.8,' I would explain that my goal was not to find a job in academia," John recalls.

"I would say, 'How many candidates worked as a research assistant for six to nine months at Purdue?' I also told them about doing landscape installation where I got to do a lot of customer service. I would also say, 'I am co-owner of Clayton Farms along with my father.' I said, 'Farming and agriculture are no different than pharmaceutical sales.' We ask, 'How do we budget our money? How do we budget our resources?'"

John further explained that, while he wasn't cut out for a more purely scientific career, he had excellent interpersonal skills and tremendous drive. These talents weren't reflected in his grades, but they were evident in the successes he'd achieved as a leader in his fraternity and elsewhere in his life. To demonstrate to his interviewer that he possessed native sales skills, he described in detail the campaign he waged to convince his "ultra-conservative" father to buy him a Camaro convertible in high school.

As he networked and interviewed, he followed up with thank-you notes, sent gift baskets of chocolates to particularly helpful representatives and built up a long list of contacts.

One of those contacts finally paid off. He had made sure to stay in touch with the Zeneca Pharmaceuticals (now AstraZeneca) representative who took him on a ride-along. Months later, when she became pregnant and moved to another state with her fiancé, she called John directly to tell him she was recommending him as her replacement. He whooped into the phone.

After a year and a half of trying, John went to work as sales representative with AstraZeneca. Eight years later, he's been promoted to a specialty sales representative selling drugs related to central nervous system care. He's as thrilled about his job as the day he started.

## John's tips

- Always be prepared for the curve ball in an interview.
- Cast the "drawbacks" on your résumé in a positive light.
- Grab any opportunity to interview, for the practice.

# Overcoming a lack of sales experience

Like John Clayton, Alexandra Olympios always knew she wanted to work in pharmaceutical sales. She got two years of initial sales training working for Automatic Data Processing (ADP) before taking a detour towards one of her other passions — gourmet cooking. She also did public relations and marketing for a line of gourmet food products sold through the Pacific Design Center in Los Angeles before embarking on a hunt for a job in the pharmaceutical world.

I met Alexandra at about this time, and I told her that one of the large pharmaceutical companies was hiring. I knew she'd have to overcome her relative lack of outside sales experience. I gave Alex a lot of advice and she took it all. She invited several working representatives out to lunch to learn more about the industry. Once she knew what position she would be interviewing for, she did something I haven't seen any other job candidate do. She drew up her own survey about the drug she hoped to be selling. She took it to local pharmacists and convinced five of them to complete it. At the bottom, she made sure each one signed his or her name. She talked with so many people about the field that she was able to walk into her interviews not only with the survey but with a 2-page list of impressive contacts. The list included personal references and all the people who had taken time to educate her about the field.

Before each interview, Alexandra read up on her prospective employer, and she role-played all her interviews with a close friend who is a Dale Carnegie instructor. Alexandra really took control of her job search. She sought out the best help she could find and marshaled it to her advantage.

Alex has now been in the industry for nearly a decade. She coaches friends about the best ways to break in. She admires those job candidates who take the time to approach her on the job. "I don't get tired of it," she says, "and I don't find it offensive. I think it takes initiative."

## Alex's tips

- Do whatever you can to stand out.
- Carry thank-you cards with you and send them immediately after each interview.

- After the interview, send your interviewer something every week to keep your name fresh in his or her mind. Alex sent thank-you cards, relevant magazine articles and emails with useful information.
- Spend a day at a populated medical building and approach representatives to introduce yourself and learn about job openings.

# The advantages of starting later in life

Kathryn Tomasewski was 48 when she started her career in pharmaceutical sales and nearly a decade later she still loves her work. "I'm passionate about it," Kathryn says.

A resident of Rockford, Illinois, Kathryn first hatched the desire to enter the profession in her early thirties but was unable to at that time because of the demands of raising her two children. Instead, she took a different job in the medical field as a medical transcriptionist. Once her kids were older, she decided to make the switch after her company stopped operating in her home town. Her breakthrough came in two phases.

Reading the classified ads in the newspaper one day, she found out about an opening in a company that offered contracted sales people to different pharmaceutical companies. Kathryn took great care in writing out a simple, clean résumé, built with plenty of active verbs.

She was called to an interview at a Marriott near O'Hare International Airport. "When I got there, my interviewer said, 'I'm a pediatrician. Sell me Tylenol.' I took a few minutes and thought it through. I think the best sale is a patient-focused sale," she says. Kathyrn asked the "doctor" what she was now prescribing to patients who come in presenting the symptom of fever. After getting a good grasp of the situation, she described the unique benefits of Tylenol. At the end, she closed by asking for a commitment to buy. Kathryn didn't have sales experience at the time, but she did well enough to receive a job offer the next day.

A couple of years later, while on her rounds, her second breakthrough opportunity presented itself. She ran into a representative from a large pharmaceutical company. She asked if there were openings and, upon learning that there were, she decided to go for it. This was before the advent of the Internet, and Kathyrn went to the library to research the company. In the interview, she made use of her research and emphasized the high value she places on integrity in her work life.

Although she was older than most candidates for pharmaceutical sales jobs, Kathryn has never felt her age was a hindrance. In fact, quite the opposite.

"The advantage is that, quite frankly, most of the physicians I visit are closer to my age than the other representatives. Some physicians have told me personally that they admire the age difference because they feel we older representatives are more seasoned. In fact, everyone in my district is in their mid-forties and older," Kathryn says.

The job does entail lifting a lot of boxes. "It's hard work," she says. Nonetheless, Kathryn plans to work straight through until she turns 70. "Then I might go part-time. I'd never want to change. I'm really content with my work. I train the new reps. I love being out in the field."

## Kathryn's tips

- Use active verbs in your résumé, and keep it short.
- Focus on the customer when you role-play a sale.
- Emphasize the value you place on integrity.
- Close well.

---

*In the following accounts, sales representatives share stories about the patients who bring meaning to their work.*

## "I am blessed"

My friend Keri Oberg's story is worth telling at some length. Keri joined Roxane/Boehringer Ingelheim as a sales representative in Los Angeles when she was 25 years old in 1993, believing she would only stay a short while. She could not have envisioned how this job would change her life.

When she first started in the position it was suggested that she visit community-based organizations (CBOs) that provided services to people living with HIV/AIDS. BI sold a product which was prescribed to AIDS patients experiencing extreme weight loss, also known as "wasting."

Not long after joining BI, Keri met Gary Costa. Gary, a gay man, was the director of a CBO called "Being Alive." Keri remembers their first meeting clearly. She was warmly welcomed by a group of individuals who appeared gaunt and were showing visible signs of Kaposi's Sarcoma lesions. She sat in Gary's office next to a poster that was both colorful and shocking. At least, it was shocking to her at the time. She considered it X-rated.

As it happens, the poster promoted safe sex. Keri later learned that people joked about the expression on her face when she saw it. Keri and Gary met several times through her initial months on the job, planning community-based programs. In the car driving to those programs, they talked. Keri asked questions she never thought she could — or would. Gary made it safe for her to learn about something she feared.

Gary became the first of many people Keri would meet who changed her mind about sexual preference and being HIV-positive. He showed her how to simply accept people for who they are. Keri learned not to focus on how people are different, but to appreciate that everyone experiences the journey of life in his or her own way.

Keri became very good friends with Gary and his partner Kyle Burton. A product Keri sold helped Kyle gain the weight he had lost during bouts of pneumonia. He was so grateful for the success he experienced on this product that he agreed to share his story through a video Keri made for a BI Sales Meeting. Kyle's health became very personal to Keri.

Unfortunately, a year later Kyle died.

Keri spent the last week of Kyle's life at the hospital with his family and Gary. "I felt so many emotions with his passing: anger, frustration, confusion and sadness," she recalls. "But I also felt inspiration. I was inspired to do more in the community for patients."

At that time, nine years ago, Keri proposed the position of HIV Community Relations to her company. BI agreed to a 6-month trial in which Keri divided her time between working with the community and continuing to cover her territory as a sales representative. She worked night and day, meeting activists nationwide and beginning the difficult task of trying to get them to see her as their advocate, not the enemy (industry).

This was a critical time as BI had just launched its first antiviral called Viramune. At the end of the trial, the position was made full-time. Today BI has a Community Relations Manager in several cities in the United States and Europe.

Other companies have followed suit and created their own Community Relations teams. Over the years, Keri has frequently been asked why this is important to the sales force of BI. She says, "I believe that sales representatives have greater success when they sell a product they believe in."

Keri made a video about why it is important that sales representatives become involved in their local communities. The video, showcased at a BI national sales meeting, was later shown via satellite to all BI operating units around the globe.

"I am blessed," Keri says. "I believed something could be done for the community, and I worked for a company that supported me in developing the concept. While there were many people at BI and in my peer group who mentored me, the real teachers have been the community activists and the patients. These individuals continue to inspire me, challenge me and make me better as a person."

Keri credits a number of individuals with having made a profound difference in her life. There was a young girl, just three years old when her photo was used in BI community advertisements. She is now 13, doing well on ARV therapy and an avid horseback rider.

There are also the HIV-positive men who sailed the "Get Challenged" boat in the Transpac race from Long Beach, California, to Hawaii. The expedition demonstrated that despite the diagnosis of HIV, one can go on to accomplish amazing things.

Another patient is a young woman who was infected with HIV at age 19. Since then, she has realized many of her dreams: hiking the entire Appalachian trail from the tip of Maine to Georgia, marrying the wonderful man who hiked with her, giving birth to two healthy little girls and starting a patient website for HIV-positive women worldwide.

Keri also thinks of all the men and women she met in Africa who grabbed her hands and thanked her when they learned she works for the company that makes Viramune.

From all of these people, Keri learned that, even with a terminal disease, one can be faithful to hope, live life and chart amazing courses for one's self and others. "I am always reminded that despite what many of us think in our youth, we are not invincible. We all make mistakes. We all take risks. And yet the outcomes make for such differing realities," Keri says.

Keri believes that she and her colleagues have done right by the HIV Community. "What a tremendous job this is!" she says. "It has its moments. They all do. Has the grass appeared greener elsewhere at times? Absolutely. But I remain mindful that not many people can make a living knowing they make a difference. I never thought I would have the chance to meet such remarkable and incredible people. Their friendships have not only changed my life, but I know they have helped me become a better person by allowing me to be a participant in their journey."

## "Hey, you saved my life."

It happens to Alex. It happens to Kathryn, too.

People see the logos on their bags and come right up and stop them. Kathryn sells Advair, a drug that helps people with asthma and chronic obstructive pulmonary disease, and Imitrex, which ameliorates migraine symptoms. "With Advair, it happens every day," Kathryn says. "They come up to me and they say, 'That drug changed my life.'"

Often, when Kathryn meets people who mention they suffer from migraines or asthma, she knows what to suggest.

Alex works often with people who are HIV-positive and who know they owe each and every day to their drug regimens. When they see the logo on her bag, they don't mince words. "People will stop me and say, 'Hey you saved my life. Your drug saved my life.' It's just one of those things where you go, 'This is why I'm here. Hey, I was here to prolong someone's life,'" Alex says. "That's why I do what I do."

## TOM'S TIP – GIVE YOURSELF A LIFT

THE FIRST INSPIRATIONAL QUOTE I recall my father giving me came from the Bible: "All things are possible for those who believe." I was in grade school at the time. This has been my personal mantra ever since.

POPS KEPT FOLDERS FILLED WITH HIS FAVORITE QUOTES. He wrote them at the top of cards he sent to friends. Like my father, I collect quotes and inspirational stories. Some sit on my computer; others hang in files. Whenever friends or colleagues are going through a trying time, I think of a quote or a story that directly applies and send it to them. I'm often surprised at how touched they say they are to receive those words right then.

I URGE OUR CANDIDATES AT TOM RUFF COMPANY to use quotes, too. An aptly chosen quote on the facing page of your brag book or at the top of a follow-up letter or handwritten note to a district manager announces your core values and indicates what sort of worker you will be. Some of our candidates send quote books along with thank-you notes to their interviewers to help with their sales talks.

I USE TIME-TESTED QUOTES AND STORIES MYSELF. Inspirational words — like those at the chapter headings throughout this book — inspire me to do more or better. When you're out there selling yourself or your product, you often need a lift. A great way to get one is to read the words of those who've triumphed over much greater obstacles.

AS ZIG ZIGLAR PUT IT, "People often say that motivation doesn't last. Well, neither does bathing. That's why we recommend it daily."

# CHAPTER EIGHTEEN

## One Doctor's View

❝ Men who are occupied in the restoration of health to other men, by the joint exertion of skill and humanity, are above all the great of the earth. They even partake of divinity, since to preserve and renew is almost as noble as to create. ❞

— Voltaire

*A doctor shares his view of the role of*
*the pharmaceutical sales representative.*

# Tom's interview with Dr. David Clayton, a physician in South Bend, Indiana:

TOM: Do you think drug reps are a valuable resource to physicians?

DR. CLAYTON: Yes, certainly. They are an excellent resource because they tell me about new drugs before I may read about them. They give me scientific articles to review as to how this particular medication may fit into my treatment plan. They are kind enough to pass along samples we can then share with our patients — particularly those who don't have drug prescription coverage or maybe are just really tight financially.

TOM: What constitutes a good pharmaceutical sales representative?

DR. CLAYTON: Someone who is conscientious about a physician's time, about my time. Whenever they see that I am busy, I prefer if they just say, "I'd be glad to leave you some samples. I'll talk to you some other time." Other days I will have up to ten minutes to talk about their product, and even their families. I think it's nice to bring up something that's personal, if possible, with the physician. That's going to generate some good will. It could be your favorite sports team, the Cubs, family and children, whatever you feel comfortable talking about is always nice. Not all of them are as sensitive as they might be, so I really value those who are.

TOM: That brings me to my next question: what constitutes a bad pharmaceutical sales representative?

DR. CLAYTON: When someone comes in and we're particularly busy and they are rude to my office staff and they take up a lot of time. They go on and on about their product. That really turns me off. The biggest turn off I've had is once a rep came in to sell a popular, but controversial, drug. It ran the risk of causing heart attacks. When I spoke with him, he said, "It's early, and they don't have any proof." I told him, "I'm going to have to wait and see how these products shake out after a lot of people have been taking them for six months to a year." I mentioned studies that had indicated some potential problems. He scoffed, as if he couldn't believe I would trust those studies. I told his peers at his company that he should never come back if they wanted me to write prescriptions for their products again.

TOM: Did you ever hear from that rep again?

DR. CLAYTON: No, no.

TOM: Do you think pharmaceutical sales is a good choice of profession?

DR. CLAYTON: Yes! I think it is an *excellent* profession, obviously to help people, and to help physicians better understand the products, to help by providing samples. Most of the pharmaceutical companies do an excellent job training their reps, not just about how to sell the products, but about how to treat patients.

TOM: How many reps call on your office on average in a week?

DR. CLAYTON: Somewhere between 20 and 25. On a full day it's not unusual to see between six to ten reps.

TOM: On average, how much time do you spend with each drug rep?

DR. CLAYTON: Around three or four minutes.

TOM: Have you ever had someone come into your office and ask either you or your office manager for referrals to drug reps to try to break into pharmaceutical sales?

DR. CLAYTON: Yes, I have had at least three that I can think of where we have handed their résumés to the reps. Reps will often bring a district manager with them, and so we have handed out résumés to the district managers, too.

TOM: Were any of those people successful in breaking into the industry?

DR. CLAYTON: Yes, two of the three.

TOM: Did they know you, or were they patients of yours, or did they come in and hand out their résumé?

DR. CLAYTON: Two of them were patients, and one was a volleyball buddy whose daughter wanted to break into pharmaceutical sales. She did get hired.

TOM: Do you think this is a good approach — to ask a physician?

DR. CLAYTON: Sure, sure. I think it's excellent because the rep hopefully has a good relationship with the doctor and the district manager. A doctor can make a strong recommendation, and the district manager is going to take a strong look at them.

TOM: What advice would you give someone who is trying to break into the industry?

DR. CLAYTON: Be honest with the doctor, respectful and smile a lot! Be friendly. It always helps to be friendly and smile.

## CHAPTER 19

# Tom's Close

**"** Never give in. Never give in. **"**

— Winston Churchill

At this point, you may reasonably be asking yourself why in the world you would want to endure the detailed research, hours of rehearsal and repeated interrogation required to land a job in pharmaceutical sales. Perhaps, once again, my friend Alexandra Olympios is the best person to provide an answer. One day, Alex, who works as a sales representative for one of the major pharmaceutical companies, sat at a coffee house with a colleague when her friend Brett walked in the door. He was downcast. He told them that his father Mel, a vibrant septuagenarian who ran three miles every day, had just been diagnosed with mesothelioma, a lung cancer caused by exposure to asbestos. The disease has a grim prognosis. Faced with news of this sort, most friends can only nod mutely, struck with the awkward knowledge that there is little they can do to help other than console. But the trio in the coffeehouse began talking. As it happens, Alex's colleague had heard that Eli Lilly was researching a new drug to treat mesothelioma. After a series of phone calls, and within only a few days, Mel began participating in drug trials for a medicine that was later approved by the Food and Drug Administration (it is now marketed under the name Alipta).

At the time, Mel was told he had only six months to live. With the help of the drug trial, he surpassed his doctor's initial predictions many times over. He lived another three years, giving him precious time with his wife and kids. "It was so exciting to know we could help," Alex says.

Pharmaceutical representatives like Alex enjoy the privilege of playing life-saving roles in the lives of patients like Brett's father. They enjoy deeply satisfying careers that enable them to help people while operating at the cutting edge of our constantly evolving biotech industry and earning top-flight livings in the process. The best pharmaceutical representatives know they get a chance, every day, to change the world for the better.

And you can, too. If you really want to. All it takes is a decision, a commitment to make a change in your own life. And a determination not to give up until you succeed.

As Winston Churchill put it, in one of my all-time favorite calls to action: "Never give in. Never give in. Never, never, never, never — in nothing, great or small, large or petty — never give in, except to convictions of honor and good sense."

It's been a pleasure sharing the most effective strategies I know for breaking into this industry. In all of your endeavors, I wish you peace, joy and success!

Sincerely,

Tom Ruff
NEW YORK CITY

*If you have a great story about how you broke in, or feedback on this book, email me at telltom@tomruff.com.*

## COMPANY PROFILES

The 12 Top Pharmaceutical Companies in Detail

Websites for Others

*The information in this section is subject to change.*

## RESOURCES:

### COMPANY WEBSITES

www.finance.yahoo.com
www.money.cnn.com/magazines/fortune
www.biz.yahoo.com
www.workingmother.com
www.pharmexec.com
www.meadjohnson.com

http://imshealth.com
www.pharmaceuticalalliance.com
www.ortho-mcneilpharmaceutical.com
www.janssen-ortho.com
www.jnj.com/innovations/pharma_pipeline/index.htm
Verispan

# Abbott Laboratories

**Abbott Laboratories**
100 Abbott Park Road
Abbott Park, IL 60064-6400
Phone: 847-937-6l00
Fax: 847-937-1511
Web Site: www.abbott.com

## HIGHLIGHTS:

- Chairman/ CEO: Miles D White
- Total Revenues 2005: $22.3 Billion
- R&D 2005: $1.8 Billion
- Sales Force Size: 3,000
- Number of Employees: 65,000
- Slogan: "A Promise for Life"
- Stock Symbol: ABT
- Ranked #93 on the 2005 Fortune 500 List of the largest U.S. based corporations in terms of revenue
- Ranked #11 of Top Pharmaceutical Companies by *Pharmaceutical Executive* magazine
- Named in 2005 by Working Mother magazine as one of the Top 10 Best Employers for Working Moms
- Named among the top employers in *Science* magazine's 2005 Top Biotech and Pharma Employers survey, for third consecutive year
- Named one of America's Most Admired Companies by *Fortune* magazine every year since 1984
- Ranked for eight consecutive years by *Fortune* magazine one of the Top Companies for Blacks and Minorities
- Pharmaceuticals sector saw 15% sales growth in 2005
- Primary products are prescription pharmaceuticals, nutritional products and diagnostic testing products
- Owns 50% TAP Pharmaceuticals Products Inc. TAP's largest selling product is Prevacid
- In 2005, Abbott diagnostics launched more than 50 new products
- Acquired Guidant's entire vascular business in April 2006, creating a new division known as Abbott Vascular
- In 2005 launched new Adult Nutrition International (ANI) division; in 2003 Abbott acquired Zone Perfect and in 2004 EAS
- In 2004 Diagnostic Products segment acquired Therasense – a leader in blood glucose self monitoring systems
- In 2004 Abbott acquired I-STAT Corp – a manufacturer blood analysis monitors
- Worldwide sales of Humira were $1.4 billion in 2005
- Set to close in the first half of 2007, Abbott agrees to sell its core laboratory diagnostics business to General Electric in 2006

## MAJOR PRODUCTS AND THERAPEUTIC AREAS:

Abbott has three segments: Pharmaceutical Products, Ross Products and International. The Pharmaceutical Products segment offers adult and pediatric pharmaceuticals for the treatment of epilepsy, migraines, bipolar disorder, dyslipidemia, rheumatoid arthritis, psoriatic arthritis, hypothyroidism, hypertension, obesity, HIV infection and hyperparathyroidism.

**Virology:** Norvir: HIV, Kaletra: HIV
**Pediatric and Neonatal:** Synagis: RSV,
**Anti-Infectives:** Biaxin, Biaxin XL, Erythromycin, PCE, Omnicef capsules, Omnicef pediatric suspension
**Metabolics:** Meridia: obesity, Synthroid: thyroid
**Neuroscience and Pain Management:** Depakote: seizures, migraines, mania, epilepsy, Depakote ER: migraine pain, mania in bipolar
**Cardiovascular:** Isoptin/Mavik: hypertension, TriCor, cholesterol and triglycerides, Tarka: hypertension
**Oncology and Renal Care:** Lupron: prostate cancer (TAP), Zemplar capsules/IV: renal
**Urology and Reproductive Health:** Hytrin: BPH,
**Gastrointestinal:** Prevacid: acid reduction (TAP), Lupron Depot
**Immunology:** Humira: moderate to severe RA-adults, psoriatic arthritis, early RA
**Perioperative and Intensive Care:** Ultane: inhal.
**Nutritional Supplements:** Ensure, Ensure Light, Glucerna, Similac, Pediasure, Isomil
**Specialty: Gengraf:** prevents organ rejection

## PIPELINE PRODUCTS:

- **Oncology:** Xinlay: prostate cancer, ABT-510, ABT-751
- **Immunology:** ABT-874: multiple sclerosis in Phase II, Humira: for ankylosing spondylitis
- **Cardiology:** Tricor in combo with a statin, Levosimendan: chronic heart failure
- **Pain Management:** Vicodin controlled release in Phase III
- **Other:** Febuxostat (TAP): chronic gout, Humira

Abbott has acquired Kos Pharmaceuticals, a specialty pharmaceutical company that develops and markets proprietary medications for the treatment of chronic cardiovascular, metabolic and respiratory diseases. With the addition of Kos, Abbott strengthens its presence in cardiovascular medicine, including lipid management.

**About the Acquisition:** On December 15, 2006, Abbott completed its acquisition of Kos Pharmaceuticals, a specialty pharmaceutical company that develops and markets proprietary medications for the treatment of chronic cardiovascular, metabolic and respiratory diseases. With the acquisition, Abbott strengthens its presence in the $20 billion lipid management market – the largest global pharmaceutical segment.

**Stronger Presence in Lipid Management:** Abbott's broad lipid management portfolio now includes:
- TriCor® (fenofibrate tablets) – a lipid-lowering agent used to treat abnormal lipid levels in the bloodstream, including cholesterol and triglycerides.
- Niaspan® (niacin extended-release tablets) – an extended-release niacin product that raises HDL, or good cholesterol levels, and also helps manage other lipids.
- Advicor® (niacin extended-release / lovastatin tablets) – a combination Niaspan / lovastatin product that treats patients with multiple lipid disorders.
- A new Niaspan Caplet Formulation is currently under U.S. Food and Drug Administration review.
- Simcor®, a fixed-dose combination of Niaspan and simvastatin (generic Zocor®), which is expected to be submitted for regulatory review in the United States in the first half of 2007.
- A next-generation fenofibrate, ABT-335, in late-stage development.
- A TriCor or ABT-335/Crestor® development program with AstraZeneca announced in July 2006.

**Additional Marketed Products:** The acquisition also brings Abbott several additional on-market products, including:
- Azmacort® (triamcinolone acetonide) – an inhaled corticosteroid used for the maintenance treatment

of asthma.
*   Cardizem® LA (diltiazem HCl) – is indicated for chronic stable angina (chest pain) and hypertension (high blood pressure).
*   Teveten® (eprosartan mesylate) / Teveten® HCT (eprosartan mesylate / hydrochlorothiazide) – are indicated for the treatment of hypertension (high blood pressure).

**In the Pipeline:** The acquisition also brings Abbott additional products in the development pipeline, including:
*   Flutiform™, currently in late-stage development for asthma
*   Icatibant, currently in late-stage development for hereditary angioedema
*   An inhaled insulin product, which will complement Abbott's significant presence in the diabetes care market.

# AstraZeneca Pharmaceuticals PLC

**AstraZeneca
Pharmaceuticals PLC**
15 Stanhope Gate
London, W1K 1LN
Fax: 44 20 7304 5151
Web Site: www.astrazeneca.com

**AstraZeneca PLC**
1800 Concord Pike
PO Box 15438
Wilmington, DE 19850-5438
US: (302) 886-3000

## HIGHLIGHTS:

*   Chairman/ CEO: David R. Brennan, (Tony Zook President & CEO, AstraZeneca US)
*   Total Revenues 2005: $23.9 Billion
*   R&D 2005: $3.4 Billion
*   12,000 researchers
*   Sales Force Size: 6,000
*   Number of Employees: 65,000 worldwide; 18,000 in the US
*   Stock Symbol: AZN
*   Formerly known as Zeneca Group PLC. Changed its name to AstraZeneca PLC in 1999
*   Ranked #6 in 2005 as one of the Top Pharmaceutical Companies (based on sales revenue) by *Pharmaceutical Executive* magazine
*   Ten of the company's products have achieved blockbuster status (sales of more than $1 billion each) including Nexium, Seroquel, Crestor, Arimidex and Symbicort
*   In 2006, for the fifth consecutive year, AstraZeneca was named a top employer and ranked fifth overall, in *Science* magazine's ranking of the world's most respected biopharmaceutical employers
*   Named in 2006 by Working Mother magazine as one of the Top 100 Best Places to Work for working mothers
*   Ranked 36th of 50 employers by *CAREERS & the disABLED Magazine* where disabled persons ranked where they would most prefer to work or believe are progressive in hiring people with disabilities
*   In 2005, National Business & Disability Council named SEROQUEL "Product of the Year", an award given to a company that is responsible for manufacturing and distributing a product that has helped enhance the lives of people with disabilities
*   In 2005, AstraZeneca company stock was selected as one of the elite Fortune 40, in a Fortune Special Investors issue
*   In 2005, included in US Black Engineer & Information Technology magazine's Most Admired Places for Minorities to Work
*   Has a strategic alliance with Cambridge Antibody Technology for discovering and developing human antibody therapeutics in inflammatory disorders.

- Has collaborations for the development of its products with various companies, including Dyax Corp.; Abgenix, Inc.; Protherics PLC; Targacept, Inc.; and AtheroGenics, Inc.
- Licensed products from Takeda Chemical Industries Ltd. (Atacand), Shionogi & Co., Ltd., (Crestor), Merck & Co. Inc., (Zestril), Sumitomo Pharmaceuticals Co., Ltd. (Merrem)

## MAJOR PRODUCTS AND THERAPEUTIC AREAS:

AstraZeneca PLC engages in the discovery, development, manufacturing and marketing of prescription pharmaceuticals primarily for the cardiovascular, gastrointestinal, neuroscience, oncology, respiratory and inflammation and infection areas in the healthcare sector worldwide. The company also has a range of therapeutic products in various development stages. In addition, AstraZeneca engages in the research, development, manufacturing and marketing of medical devices and implants for use in healthcare, primarily in urology surgery and odontology.

**Cardiovascular:** CRESTOR: synthetic lipid-lowering agent, or (HMG-CoA ) reductase inhibitor, commonly known as a statin, ATACAND: angiotensin II receptor blocker (ARB) for the treatment of hypertension, ATACAND HCT: combination agent of an ARB and a diuretic for the treatment of hypertension, TOPROL-XL: a beta1-selective (cardioselective) adrenoceptor-blocking agent for hypertension, the long term treatment of angina pectoris and stable, symptomatic (NYHA Class II or III) heart failure of ischemic, hypertensive or cardiomyopathic origin, PLENDIL: calcium channel antagonist for the treatment of hypertension, ZESTRIL: a long-acting angiotensin converting enzyme (ACE) inhibitor for the treatment of hypertension and adjunctive therapy in the management of heart failure in patients who are not responding adequately to diuretics and digitalis and for the treatment of hemodynamically stable patients within 24 hours of an acute myocardial infarction to improve survival (lost US patent 2003, now generic), ZESTORETIC: a combination agent that combines an (ACE) inhibitor and a diuretic for the treatment of hypertension, LEXXEL: a combination product, consisting of an outer layer of enalapril maleate (ACE inhibitor) surrounding a core tablet of an extended-release felodipine formulation (dihydropyridine calcium channel blocker) and used to treat hypertension, TENORETIC: a combination product, consisting of a beta$_1$-selective (cardioselective) blocking agent and a monosulfonamyl diuretic for the treatment of hypertension, TENORMIN (I.V. injection/Tablets): a beta$_1$-selective (cardioselective) adrenoreceptor-blocking agent for the management of hypertension and the long-term management of angina pectoris and the management of hemodynamically stable patients with definite or suspected acute myocardial infarction to reduce cardiovascular mortality
**Neuroscience:** SEROQUEL: for treating schizophrenia and the short-term treatment of acute manic episodes associated with bipolar I disorder (in adults over the age of eighteen), ZOMIG (tablets, disintegrating tablets and nasal spray): for the acute treatment of migraine with or without aura in adults, NAROPIN INJECTION: a long acting local anesthetic for the production of local or regional anesthesia for surgery, for postoperative pain management and for obstetrical procedures DIPRIVAN INJECTABLE EMULSION: an intravenous sedative hypnotic agent for the induction and maintenance of anesthesia in adults and children 3 years of age and older, for initiation and maintenance of monitored anesthesia care (MAC) sedation during diagnostic procedures in adults and for intensive care unit (ICU) sedation in intubated mechanically ventilated adults
**Oncology:** ARIMIDEX: for adjuvant treatment (treatment following surgery with or without radiation) of postmenopausal women with hormone receptor-positive early breast cancer, for first-line treatment (first hormonal treatment in advanced breast cancer) for postmenopausal women with hormone receptor-positive or hormone receptor-unknown locally advanced or metastatic breast cancer and for treatment of advanced breast cancer in postmenopausal women with disease progression following tamoxifen therapy, FASLODEX: for the treatment of hormone receptor positive metastatic breast cancer in postmenopausal women with disease progression following antiestrogen therapy, CASODEX: for use in combination therapy with a luteinizing hormone-releasing hormone analog (LHRH-A) for the treatment of Stage D2 metastatic carcinoma of the prostate, Zoladex: for the palliative treatment of advanced carcinoma of the prostate and for use in combination with flutamide for the management of locally confined stage T2b-T4 (Stage B2-C) carcinoma of the prostate, IRESSA: for the continued treatment of patients with locally advanced or metastatic non–small-cell lung cancer (NSCLC) after failure of both platinum-based and docetaxel chemotherapies who are benefiting or have benefited from Iressa, NOLVADEX (TAMOXIFEN): to reduce the incidence of breast cancer, only in women at high-risk, ("High risk" is defined as women at least 35 years of age with a 5-year predicted risk of breast cancer > 1.67%, as calculated by the Gail Model), also for use in women with Ductal Carcinoma in Situ (DCIS),

following breast surgery and radiation, as it reduces the risk of invasive breast cancer, also reduces the occurrence of contralateral breast cancer in patients receiving adjuvant Nolvadex for breast cancer, also for the treatment of node-positive breast cancer in postmenopausal women following total mastectomy or segmental mastectomy, axillary dissection, breast irradiation and for the treatment of axillary node-negative breast cancer in women following total mastectomy or segmental mastectomy, axillary dissection and breast irradiation

**Gastrointestinal:** NEXIUM: a proton pump inhibitor (PPI) for heartburn and other symptoms associated with gastroesophageal reflux disease (GERD) and for the healing of erosive esophagitis, also for maintenance of healing of erosive esophagitis and, in combination with amoxicillin and clarithromycin, for eradication of *Helicobacter pylori* infection in patients with duodenal ulcer disease, PRILOSEC: an acid PPI available as delayed-release capsules, for heartburn and other symptoms associated with GERD, erosive esophagitis, maintenance of healed erosive esophagitis, active duodenal ulcer, active benign gastric ulcer, pathological hypersecretory conditions and in combination with clarithromycin and amoxicillin or with clarithromycin for Helicobacter pylori- associated duodenal ulcer disease

**Respiratory and Inflammation:** PULMICORT TURBUHALER: is an inhaled corticosteroid for maintenance treatment of asthma as prophylactic therapy in adult and pediatric patients six years of age and older, also for patients requiring oral corticosteroid therapy for asthma, PULMICORT RESPULES: inhalation suspension for the maintenance treatment of asthma and as prophylactic therapy in children 12 months to 8 years of age, RHINOCORT AQUA: for the treatment of nasal symptoms of seasonal and perennial allergic rhinitis in patients 6 years and older, ACCOLATE: nonsteroidal tablet for the prevention and continuous treatment of asthma in adults and children 5 years of age and older

**Infection:** MERREM IV: for the treatment of the following infections: Intra-abdominal infections, complicated appendicitis and peritonitis caused by viridans group streptococci, Escherichia coli, Klebsiella pneumoniae, Pseudomonas aeruginosa, Bacteroides fragilis, B thetaiotaomicron and Peptostreptococcus species, and for Bacterial Meningitis (pediatric patients greater than or equal to 3 months only) Bacterial meningitis caused by Streptococcus pneumoniae, Haemophilus influenzae (b-lactamase and non-b lactamase-producing strains) and Neisseria meningitides, CEFOTAN INJECTION: a broad spectrum cephalosporin antibiotic used to treat a wide range of bacterial infections

## PIPELINE PRODUCTS:

- Exanta: anti-clotting agent, for the treatment of diseases associated with blood clots, would be the only agent besides warfarin for this type use (2004 US FDA denied it due to some liver issues, but it has been approved in Europe)
- Galida: (Phase III) PPAR agonist for insulin resistance and lipid abnormalities associated with type 2 diabetes
- AZD6140: anti-platelet therapy (Phase II)
- AZD0837 and AZD9684: thrombosis (Phase II)
- AZD7009: anti-arrhythmic to restore normal heart rhythm in patients with atrial fibrillation
- AZD0865: new class of drug, potassium-competitive acid blockers (P-CAB), for GERD (Phase II)
- AZD3355/AZD9343: reflux inhibitors
- AZD7371: treating functional GI diseases (Phase II)
- AZD8129: depression and anxiety (Phase II)
- AZD4282/AZD9272/AZD6538: neuropathic pain
- Cerovive: acute ischaemic stroke
- AZD7371: overactive bladder (Phase II)
- AZD1080: Alzheimer's disease
- AZD3102: human monoclonal antibodies
- AZD5904: multiple sclerosis
- ZD6474: anti-cancer agent (Phase II)
- ZD6126/AZD4440: vascular targeting agent (Phase II)
- ZD4054: inhibits tumor cell proliferation (granted fast track designation by the US FDA)
- AZD9056: for osteoarthritis and rheumatoid arthritis (Phase II)
- Seven new compounds in preclinical stage for COPD, asthma and rhinitis, osteoarthritis and rheumatoid arthritis
- Additionally, there are many line extensions being submitted to the FDA for additional indications on currently marketed products

# Bristol-Myers Squibb Co.

**Bristol-Myers Squibb Co.**
345 Park Avenue
New York, NY 10154
Phone: 212-546-4000
Fax: 212-546-4020
Web Site: www.bms.com

## HIGHLIGHTS:

- Interim CEO: James M. Cornelius
- Total Revenues 2005: $19.2 Billion
- R&D 2005: $2.7 Billion
- 5,400 researchers
- Sales Force Size: Not available
- Number of Employees: 42,000
- Stock Symbol: BMY
- Formerly known as Bristol-Myers Company and changed its name to Bristol-Myers Squibb Company in 1989
- In Feb 2005, ranks among the world's 100 most sustainable corporations at the World Economic Forum
- Ranked #110 out of top 500 companies by revenues by *Fortune* magazine
- Ranked #8 of top pharmaceutical companies by *Pharmaceutical Executive* magazine
- Plavix is the #2 brand worldwide; in 2005 reached $3.8 Billion in sales
- *Working Mother* magazine's Top 100 Best Companies, for ninth consecutive year in 2006
- Bristol-Myers Squibb has strategic alliances with Sanofi-Aventis; Otsuka Pharmaceutical Co., Ltd.; and ImClone Systems Incorporated
- Nominated by National Association for Female Executives' (NAFE) annual list of Top 30 Companies for Executive Women
- In 2005, won the Lance Armstrong Foundation award for providing cancer therapies free of charge to tens of thousands of low-income patients
- Had six new medications gain regulatory approval from Nov 2002 to Dec 2005, more than any other pharmaceutical company in the United States during that time period
- Have taken an aggressive industry approach to voluntarily forgo all direct-to-consumer advertising of new products for up to a year following introduction into the marketplace to give doctors time to learn about the medications before they are promoted to the general public; first pharmaceutical company to take this ethical approach

## MAJOR PRODUCTS AND THERAPEUTIC AREAS:

Bristol-Myers Squibb has three segments: Pharmaceuticals, Nutritionals and other Healthcare. The Pharmaceuticals segment provides products for cardiovascular; virology, including immunology; infectious diseases; oncology; affective disorders; and metabolics. It also offers various pain relief products in Europe. The Nutritionals segment manufactures, markets, distributes and sells infant formulas and other nutritional products. The other Healthcare segment provides ostomy, wound- and skin-care products; medical imaging products that primarily include cardiac perfusion imaging agents and ultrasound contrast agents; and other consumer medicines.

**Cardiovascular:** PLAVIX: antiplatelet medication (co-promote with Sanofi-Aventis), PRAVACHOL: cholesterol, Avalide®/Avapro®: hypertension, COUMADIN: prophylaxis and/or treatment of venous thrombosis and its extension, and pulmonary embolism, prophylaxis and/or treatment of the thromboembolic complications associated with atrial fibrillation and/or cardiac valve replacement; to reduce the risk of death, recurrent myocardial infarction and thromboembolic events such as stroke or systemic embolization after myocardial infarction

**Infectious Diseases:** Baraclude™: chronic hepatitis B virus (HBV) infection in adults, Reyataz®: used in combination with other medicines to treat human immunodeficiency virus (HIV), Sustiva®: used in combination with other antiretroviral agents for the treatment of HIV-1 infection, Tequin®: fluoroquinolone anti-infective for lung, sinus, skin, UTIs and STDs, Videx®: infectious disease, Zerit® (also known as d4T): infectious disease
**Metabolics/Diabetes:** Glucophage® XR, diabetes, Glucovance®: diabetes, Metaglip: diabetes, Sinemet® CR: nervous system
**Virology/Immunology:** Orencia®: moderate to severe rheumatoid arthritis (launch 2006)
Oncology: Erbitux®: for patients with head and neck cancer whose tumor has grown or spread to other parts of the body after receiving chemotherapy; or in combination with radiation therapy, for the treatment of early stages of most types of head and neck cancer
Mental Disorders: ABILIFY®: schizophrenia and bipolar disorders, EMSAM: patch for adults with major depressive disorder (launch 2006)
**Nutritionals:** ENFAMIL: infant formula; plus all other Mead Johnson infant nutritional products (Mead Johnson is part of Bristol-Myers Squibb Company's Nutritional segment)

## PIPELINE PRODUCTS:

BMS has more than 50 compounds in development in the following critical disease areas: affective (psychiatric) disorders, Alzheimer's disease, atherosclerosis and thrombosis, cancer, diabetes, hepatitis, HIV/AIDS, obesity, rheumatoid arthritis and solid organ transplantation. Ten compounds are currently in late-stage Full Development, including four now in the regulatory approval process.
* DASATINIB: chronic myelogenous leukemia, as well as Philadelphia chromosome-positive (Ph+) acute lymphoblastic leukemia, in adult patients (FDA grants priority review March 2006)
* PARGLUVA: Type 2 diabetes (FDA wants more studies completed)
* SAXAGLIPTIN: Type 2 diabetes (Phase III)
* IXABEPILONE: Cancer (Phase III)
* IPILIMUMAB: Cancer (Phase III)
* VINFLUNINE: Cancer (Phase III)
* BELATACEPT: prevention of solid organ transplantation rejection (Phase III)

# Eli Lilly & Co.

**Eli Lilly & Co.**
Lilly Corporate Center
Indianapolis, IN 46285
Phone: 317-276-2000
Fax: 317-276-4878
Web Site: www.lilly.com

## HIGHLIGHTS:

* Chairman/ CEO: Sidney Taurel
* Total Revenues 2005: $14.6 Billion
* R&D 2005: $ 3.1 Billion
* 8,317 researchers
* Sales Force Size: Not available
* Number of Employees: 41,800
* Stock Symbol: LLY
* Ranked #148 out of top 500 companies in terms of revenue by *Fortune* magazine
* *Fortune* magazine ranked Lilly in the 100 Best Companies to Work For in America,    Global Most

Admired Companies and 50 Best Companies for Minorities
- *Money* magazine rewarded Lilly for having America's Best Company Benefits
- *Science* magazine recognized Lilly as one of the Best Companies for Scientists
- *Industry Week* recognized Lilly's management with 100 Best-Managed Companies
- *Business Ethics* magazine rewarded Lilly under 100 Best Corporate Citizens
- Ranked #10 of Top Pharmaceutical Companies (based on sales revenue) by *Pharmaceutical Executive* magazine
- *Working Mother* magazine's Top 10 Best Places to Work (in the top 10 for the seventh time in 11 years)
- Zyprexa ranks 7th in worldwide global pharmaceutical sales
- Co-promotes products with Takeda (Actos), Quintiles (Cymbalta) and Boehringer Ingelheim (Yentreve)
- Has a joint venture with biotech partner ICOS Corporation who developed the Cialis molecule
- Shares recent and ongoing research and development with partners: Alkermes, Merck KGaA and Structural GenomiX
- In 2003, started an important, multi-pronged, philanthropic, public-private partnership to address the expanding global crisis of multi-drug-resistant tuberculosis (MDR-TB). Every year, in developing countries about 2 million people die from tuberculosis, a curable disease. In their lifetime, those infected with the disease also pass it on to another 20 people. Lilly and partners are working with the World Health Organization to help address this pandemic.

**MAJOR PRODUCTS AND THERAPEUTIC AREAS:**

Eli Lilly and Company, through its subsidiaries, engages in the discovery, development, manufacture and sale of pharmaceutical and animal health products in the United States and internationally. In the pharmaceutical sector, Eli Lilly offers primarily neuroscience, endocrine and oncology products.

**Neuroscience:** Zyprexa: schizophrenia, bipolar mania and bipolar maintenance; Cymbalta: depression and diabetic peripheral neuropathic pain (co-promote with Quintiles); Strattera: attention-deficit hyperactivity disorder in children, adolescents and adults; Prozac: depression and bulimia and obsessive-compulsive disorders; Permax: Parkinson's disease; Sarafem: pre-menstrual dysphoric disorders (PMDD); Symbyax: bipolar depression; Yentreve: stress urinary incontinence (co-promote with Boehringer Ingelheim)
**Endocrine/Diabetes:** Humalog, Humalog Mix 75/25, Humalog Mix 50/50 and Humulin: diabetes; Actos: type 2 diabetes (co-promote with Takeda), Byetta: type 2 diabetes; Evista: prevention and treatment of osteoporosis in post-menopausal women; Humatrope: human growth hormone deficiency and idiopathic short stature; Forteo: severe osteoporosis in women and men, stimulates new bone formation
**Oncology:** Gemzar: pancreatic cancer; Alimta: malignant pleural mesothelioma and non-small cell lung cancer
**Urology:** Cialis®: distinctive new treatment for erectile dysfunction
**Infectious Disease:** Xigris®: first treatment approved for adult severe-sepsis patients at a high risk of death

**PIPELINE PRODUCTS:**

- Arxxant: will be first product to treat moderate to severe non-proliferative diabetic retinopathy (Phase III; submitted to FDA)
- Prasugrel: for acute coronary syndrome (Phase III, in collaboration w/ Sankyo Pharmaceuticals)
- Enzastaurin: cancer, brain tumors, non-Hodgkin's lymphoma
- Arzoxifene: osteoporosis and risk reduction of breast cancer
- Inhaled Insulin: diabetes (in collaboration with Alkermes)

# Forest Laboratories, Inc.

**Forest Laboratories, Inc.**
909 Third Avenue
New York, NY 10022-4731
Phone: 212-421-7850
Fax: 212-750-9152
Web Site: www.frx.com

## HIGHLIGHTS:

* Chairman/ CEO: Howard Solomon
* Total Revenues 2006: $2.78 Billion
* R&D 2005: $410 million
* 1,000 researchers
* Sales Force Size: 2,800
* Number of Employees: 5,136
* Stock Symbol: FRX
* One of the smallest companies in the industry and is known to take very good care of its employees with benefits programs and stock options
* Ranked #588 out of Top 1000 Companies in terms of revenues by *Fortune* magazine
* Listed on the *Forbes* Platinum list of the 400 Best Companies in America for each of the past three years, with special recognition as the best managed company in the Drug and Biotechnology industry in 2004
* Ranked #15 of Top Pharmaceutical Companies in terms of sales revenue by *Pharmaceutical Executive* magazine
* *Working Mother* magazine's Top 100 Best Places to Work for working mothers
* In 2006, *Pharmaceutical Executive* magazine ranked Forest #3 of all pharmaceutical companies for its strategic industry audit
* Has strategic alliances with: Sankyo Co., Ltd. in Japan, Gedeon Richter Ltd., in Hungary, Merck KgaA, in Germany, Pierre Fabre Pharmaceuticals, in France, Rotta Research Laboratorium, in Italy, H. Lundbeck A/S, in Denmark, Glenmark Pharmaceuticals, in India, Merz & Co., GmbH, in Germany and Recordati S.p.A., in Italy.
* Works closely with several American companies, such as Cypress Biosciences and ChemoCentryx for the joint development of future products
* Forest and Almirall, a privately held pharmaceutical company headquartered in Barcelona, Spain, have entered an agreement to develop, market and distribute Almirall's novel inhaled, long-acting muscarinic antagonist, LAS34273, in the United States, for chronic obstructive pulmonary disease (COPD). The product is being developed in a Multi Dose-Dry Powder Inhaler (MDPI) which represents an improvement in drug delivery over currently available devices.

## MAJOR PRODUCTS AND THERAPEUTIC AREAS:

Forest Laboratories, Inc. engages in the development, manufacture and sale of both branded and generic forms of ethical drug products, as well as nonprescription pharmaceutical products sold over-the-counter. The company's products focus on central nervous system, pain management, respiratory, obgyn/pediatrics, endocrinology and cardiovascular treatments. The company markets its products directly and though independent distributors worldwide to physicians, pharmacies, hospitals, managed care and other healthcare organizations.

**Central Nervous System:** Campral: for the maintenance of abstinence from alcohol in patients with alcohol dependence, Namenda: an N-methyl-D-aspartate-receptor antagonist, is used for the treatment of moderate to severe Alzheimer's disease, Lexapro: for the initial and maintenance treatment of depressive disorders and for generalized anxiety disorders, Celexa: for depression and anxiety disorders
**Pain Management:** Combunox: an opioid and NSAID combination, for the short-term management of pain, to help manage acute, moderate to severe pain for up to seven days, CCR1 is a chemokine

receptor involved in the inflammation process

**Cardiovascular:** Tiazac: a calcium channel blocker, lowers blood pressure by blocking calcium influx into the smooth muscle cells of the blood vessels, Benicar: for hypertension, lowers blood pressure by blocking the angiotensin II receptor and interrupting the release of the hormone which causes salt retention and increased blood volume, BENICAR HCT combines BENICAR with the diuretic (water pill) hydrochlorothiazide for additional blood pressure lowering

**Respiratory:** Aerobid: provides metered-dose inhaler medication to help manage the inflammation caused by asthma, AeroChamber Plus: a holding chamber device designed to maximize the delivery of metered-dose inhaler medications to patients' lungs

**ObGyn/Pediatrics:** Cervidil Vaginal Insert: a removable product for ripening the cervix, the process by which the cervix becomes more compliant and which must take place before induction can be safely undertaken, Infasurf: for respiratory distress syndrome (RDS), a lung condition that can occur in premature infants whose lungs have not completely developed

**Endocrinology:** ARMOUR THYROID: combination therapy of $T_4$ (levothyroxine sodium) and $T_3$ (L-triiodothyronine), a natural preparation derived from porcine thyroid glands, for the treatment of hypothyroidism, LEVOTHROID: a synthetic product containing the hormone levothyroxine $(T_4)$, used to treat various thyroid disorders like hypothyroidism, THYROLAR: only synthetic product combining L-triiodothyronine $(T_3)$ and levothyroxine sodium $(T_4)$ indicated for the treatment of hypothyroidism.

## PIPELINE PRODUCTS:

* Replidyne and Forest announced in February 2006, FDA acceptance for review of New Drug Application for oral antibiotic Faropenem Medoxomil for acute bacterial sinusitis, community-acquired pneumonia, acute exacerbation of chronic bronchitis, uncomplicated skin and skin structure infections
* Milnacipran is in Phase III development for the treatment of fibromyalgia syndrome
* RGH-188 in Phase I clinical trials, an atypical antipsychotic for the treatment of schizophrenia, bipolar mania and other psychiatric conditions
* memantine for neuropathic pain, in Phase II
* dexloxiglumide for gastrointestinal disorders, in Phase II
* dneramexane for several CNS indications, in Phase II
* Desmoteplase, a novel plasminogen activator, or blood clot-dissolving agent, for stroke, Phase II
* GRC 3886, a novel, orally available Phosphodiesterase-IV inhibitor in development for chronic obstructive pulmonary disorder and asthma, in phase I
* RGH-188, for schizophrenia, in Phase I
* partnership with ChemoCentryx, which is developing novel anti-inflammatories and is in the preclinical stage

# GlaxoSmithKline plc

**GlaxoSmithKline plc**
980 Great West Road
Brentford, TW8 9GS
United Kingdom
Phone: 44 20 8047 5000
Fax: 44 20 8047 7807
Web Site: www.gsk.com
US: 888-825-5249

**HIGHLIGHTS:**

- Chairman/ CEO: JP Garnier
- Total Revenues 2005: $37.6 Billion
- R&D 2005: $5.47 Billion
- 15,000 researchers
- Sales Force Size: 10,000
- Number of Employees: 100,728
- Stock Symbol: GSK
- In Dec. 2000, GSK was born from the merger/acquisition of Glaxo Wellcome plc and SmithKline Beecham plc, both large English pharmaceutical companies
- In Sept. 2005, GSK held second position in the world pharmaceutical market with a market share of 6.3%, behind Pfizer at 8.9%. GSK had 8 of the world's top 60 pharmaceutical products: Avandia, Flonase, Imitrex, Lamictal, Advair, Paxil, Wellbutrin and Zofran.
- Ranked #2 of Top Pharmaceutical Companies in terms of sales revenue by *Pharmaceutical Executive* magazine
- *Working Mother* magazine's Top 100 Best Places to Work for working mothers, for fifth year in a row
- In 2006, GlaxoSmithKline and Sirna Therapeutics announce major alliance in RNAi-based therapeutics for respiratory disease
- Has a strategic alliance with Theravance, Inc. to develop and commercialize medicines across various therapeutic areas; and partnerships with the Aeras Global TB Vaccine Foundation and the International AIDS Vaccine Initiative

**MAJOR PRODUCTS AND THERAPEUTIC AREAS:**

GlaxoSmithKline PLC engages in the creation, discovery, development, manufacture and marketing of pharmaceutical and consumer health related products worldwide. The company operates in two segments, Pharmaceuticals and Consumer Healthcare. The Pharmaceuticals segment manufactures prescription drugs in various areas principally comprising respiratory, central nervous system, antivirals, antibacterials, antimalarials, metabolic, oncology and emesis and cardiovascular and urogenital diseases. It also manufactures various vaccines, such as hepatitis A, hepatitis B, diphtheria, tetanus, whooping cough, measles, mumps, rubella, polio, typhoid, influenza and bacterial meningitis. The Consumer Healthcare segment produces over-the-counter medicines, such as analgesics, dermatologicals, gastro intestinal, respiratory tract, smoking control and natural wellness support products; oral care, including toothpastes and mouthwashes, as well as various toothbrushes and denture care products; and nutritional healthcare products comprising Lucozade glucose energy and sports drinks, as well as Ribena, a blackcurrant juice-based drink with vitamin C, and Horlicks, a range of milk-based malted food and chocolate drinks. Some commonly known consumer products are: Abreva, Aquafresh, Binaca, Citrucel, Contac, Ecotrin, Nicorette/Nicoderm CQ, Poilgrip, Sensodyne, Tagamet and Tums.

**Respiratory:** ADVAIR DISKUS: to treat asthma and chronic obstructive pulmonary disease (COPD) associated with chronic bronchitis, FLOVENT: inhaled steroids for treating the inflammation associated with asthma and COPD, SEREVENT: long acting bronchodilator to treat asthma and COPD, FLONASE: steroid intra-nasal preparations for treating perennial and seasonal rhinitis
**Central Nervous System:** PAXIL: for treating depression, panic, obsessive compulsive disorder, post traumatic stress disorder, social anxiety disorder, premenstrual dysphoric disorder and generalized anxiety disorder, WELLBUTRIN: anti-depressant, IMITREX: severe or frequent migraines and cluster headaches, AMERGE: for treating migraines, LAMICTAL: for treating epilepsy and bipolar disorder, REQUIP: for treating Parkinson's disease and Restless Leg Syndrome (RLS)
**Antivirals:** AGENERASE: antiviral protease inhibitor (PI) for treating HIV, COMBIVAR: combination product of lamivudine and zidovudine (Retrovir and Epivir) used with other antiretrovirals for the treatment of HIV-1, ZIAGEN: HIV treatment, TRIZIVIR: Combivir plus Ziagen for treating HIV, EPZICOM: Epivir and Ziagen combo pill for HIV/AIDS, LEXIVA: a protease inhibitor to treat HIV, ZEFFIX: for treating chronic hepatitis B, VALTREX: for treating, suppressing and reducing the transmission of genital herpes, cold sores, shingles and chicken pox
**Antibacterials:** AMOXIL: penicillin antibiotic for treating bacterial infections, AUGMENTIN ES/XR:

a combination antibiotic of amoxicillin and clavulanic acid for treating bacterial infections of the sinus, throat, ears, skin, lungs, animal bites, used in both children and adults, BACTROBAN CREAM/OINTMENT/NASAL OINTMENT: antibacterial for skin and wound infections and bacteria in the nose, CEPTAZ INJECTION: antibiotic for major systemic infections like lower respiratory tract, urinary, skin, bone and joint, intra-abdominal and gynecological infections, also for bacterial septicemia and CNS infections like meningitis

**Antimalarials:** MALARONE: for treating certain strains of malaria, LAPDAP: for treating malaria

**Oncology and Emesis:** ZOFRAN: to prevent nausea and vomiting after chemotherapy, radiotherapy and surgery, HYCAMTIN: second line treatment for both ovarian cancer and small cell lung cancer, BEXXAR: for patients with CD20 follicular non-Hodgkin's lymphoma whose disease is refractory to rituximab and who have relapsed following chemotherapy

**Metabolic:** AVANDIA: type 2 diabetes medication, AVANDAMET: combination of Avandia and metformin used for anti-diabetic medication, AVANDARYL: a combo product of Avandia and Amaryl (a Sanofi-Aventis product) used to treat diabetes, BONIVA: for post menopausal osteoporosis

**Cardiovascular:** COREG: for the treatment of essential hypertension, for the treatment of mild to severe heart failure of ischemic or cardiomyopathic origin and to reduce cardiac mortality who have survived a myocardial infarction and have a left ventricular ejection fraction less than or equal to 40%

**Urogenital:** AVODART: for treating enlarged prostate, LEVITRA: for male erectile dysfunction

**Anti-inflammatory:** BETNOVATE: anti-inflammatory steroid products used to treat skin diseases, such as eczema and psoriasis, ACLOVATE CREAM/OINTMENT: relief from inflammatory and pruritic dermatoses, CUTIVATE CREAM/OINTMENT: corticosteroid for inflammatory and pruritic dermatoses

**Nonsteroidal anti-inflammatory:** RELAFEN: a nonsteroidal anti-inflammatory drug for the treatment of arthritis

**Gastrointestinal:** ZANTAC: peptic ulcer disease and various gastric acid related disorders, TAGAMET: to treat ulcers and gastroesophageal reflux disease (GERD)

## PIPELINE PRODUCTS:

Has one of largest pipelines in industry, 149 projects as of Feb 2006: 95 are new chemical entities, 29 are product line extensions, 25 vaccines, 8 new products to enter Phase III in 2006, which doubles their late stage development pipeline.

- AVANDAMET XR: PPAR gamma agonist plus metformin for type 2 diabetes (Phase III)
- AVANDIA + SIMVASTATIN: PPAR gamma agonist + statin for type 2 diabetes (Phase II)
- AVANDARYL: PPAR gamma agonist + sulphonylurea for type 2 diabetes (has been accepted by the FDA)
- DARAPLADIB: Lp-PLA2 inhibitor for atherosclerosis (Phase II/III)
- ARIXTRA: synthetic factor Xa inhibitor for the treatment of acute coronary syndrome (Phase III)
- Coreg CR: a beta blocker for hypertension and congestive heart failure (at FDA)
- ETAQUINE: for malaria (Phase III)
- Altabax (retapamulin): topical pleuromutilin for bacterial skin infections (at FDA)
- CHLORPROGUANIL, DAPSONE + ARTESUNATE (CDA): treatment of uncomplicated malaria (Phase III)
- ENTEREG: peripheral mu-opioid antagonist for opioid induced GI symptoms (Phase III)
- AVODART: 5-alpha reductase inhibitor for reduction in risk of prostate cancer (Phase III)
- AVODART + ALPHA BLOCKER: for benign prostatic hyperplasia (Phase
- BRECANAVIR: aspartyl protease inhibitor for HIV infections (Phase II)
- RELENZA: neuraminidase inhibitor for influenza prophylaxis (at FDA)
- ELTROMBOPAG: thrombopoietin agonist for thrombocytopaenia (Phase III)
- TYKERB: ErbB-2 and epidermal growth factor receptor (EGFR) dual kinase inhibitor for breast, renal, head and neck cancers (Phase III)
- HYCAMTIN: topo-isomerase I inhibitor, first-line therapy for ovarian cancer, also second-line therapies for small cell lung cancer and cervical cancer (Phase III)
- ARRANON: guanine arabinoside prodrug for acute lymphoblastic leukemia and lymphomas (Approved recently by FDA)
- AVAMYS/ALLERMIST: glucocorticoid agonist for allergic rhinitis (Phase III)
- SERETIDE/ADVAIR: beta2 agonist/inhaled corticosteroid for COPD (Phase III)

- SERETIDE/ADVAIR: beta2 agonist/inhaled corticosteroid for asthma using a non-CFC inhaler (Approved recently by FDA)
- SERETIDE: beta2 agonist/inhaled corticosteroid for initial maintenance therapy in asthma (at FDA)
- ARIFLO: PDE IV inhibitor (oral) for COPD (at FDA)

# Johnson & Johnson

**Johnson & Johnson**
One Johnson & Johnson Plaza
New Brunswick, NJ 08933
Phone: 732-524-0400
Fax: 732-214-0332
Web Site: www.jnj.com

## HIGHLIGHTS:

- Chairman/ CEO: William C. Weldon
- Total Revenues 2005: $50.5 Billion
- R&D 2005: $6.5 Billion
- 4,000 researchers
- Sales Force Size: 5,500
- Number of Employees: 117,500
- Stock Symbol: JNJ
- Ranked #32 out of Top 500 Companies in terms of revenue by *Fortune* magazine
- Ranked #4 of Top Pharmaceutical Companies by *Pharmaceutical Executive* magazine
- With $17.2 billion in pharmaceutical sales in 2005 coming from more than 100 medicines marketed in 175 countries, Johnson & Johnson is the fastest growing of the top 10 pharmaceutical companies, according to Independent Market Research (IMR)
- Five of the company's products have achieved blockbuster status (sales of more than $1 billion each), with four more having sales exceeding $500 million
- Pharmaceuticals represent 59 percent of total Johnson & Johnson revenue
- *Working Mother* magazine's Top 10 Best Places to Work for working mothers
- Johnson & Johnson's pharmaceutical companies are considered a family of companies and include: ALZA Corp, Centocor Inc, Janssen-Cilag, Janssen Pharmaceutica Products L.P., Ortho Biotech Products L.P., Ortho-McNeil Pharmaceutical Inc, Scios Inc, Tibotec and Tibotec Therapeutics
- The most broadly based health-care-products company in the world and is operating in more than 175 countries
- Acquired Pfizer's Consumer Healthcare Division in 2006

## MAJOR PRODUCTS AND THERAPEUTIC AREAS:

Johnson and Johnson has three segments: Consumer, Pharmaceutical and Medical Devices and Diagnostics (MDD). The Consumer segment manufactures and markets a range of products used in the baby and child care, skin care, oral and wound care and women's health care fields, as well as nutritional and over-the-counter pharmaceutical products. Well known products are: AVEENO, BAND-AID, CAREFREE, CLEAN & CLEAR, JOHNSON'S, PEPCID, NEUTROGENA, SPLENDA, STAYFREE and TYLENOL brands. The Pharmaceutical segment has various therapeutic areas, including anti fungal, anti-infective, cardiovascular, contraceptive, dermatology, gastrointestinal, hematology, immunology, neurology, oncology, pain management, psychotropic and urology.

**Anti-Infectives/Anti Fungal:** LEVAQUIN: fluoroquinolone anti-infective (Ortho-McNeil/Daiichi Pharmaceutical), NIZORAL: antifungal (McNeil), SPECTAZOLE: antifungal (Ortho-McNeil), SPORANOX: antifungal (Ortho-McNeil)

**Neuroscience, Psychotropic and Pain Management:** CONCERTA: ADHD, REMICADE: Crohn's disease in adults, rheumatoid arthritis, ankylosing spondylitis, psoriatic arthritis, ulcerative colitis (Centocor/Janssen), RISPERDAL CONSTA injection for schizophrenia (Janssen), RISPERDAL: antipsychotic (Janssen), REMINYL: Alzheimer's disease (Janssen/Shire Pharmaceuticals), DURAGESIC: treatment of chronic, moderate to severe pain (ALZA/Janssen), ORTHOVICS: pain in osteoarthritis (OA) of the knee (Ortho Biotech), TOPAMAX anti-epilepsy (Ortho-McNeil), AXERT: migraines (Janssen-Ortho)

**Cardiovascular:** NATRECOR acute congestive heart failure (Scios), RETAVASE: acute myocardial infarction (AMI)/heart attack (Scios), ReoPro: prevention of cardiac ischemic complications (Centocor)

**Dermatology:** ORTHO TRI-CYCLEN: first oral contraceptive for a non-contraceptive indication-acne (Ortho-McNeil)

**Gastrointestinal:** ACIPHEX gastrointestinal disorders (Janssen/Eisai/Ortho-McNeil)

**Oncology/Hematology/ Immunology:** PROCRIT/EPREX: anemia(Ortho Biotech), LEUSTATIN: for a rare form of cancer called hairy cell leukemia (Ortho Biotech), ORTHOCLONE OKT 3: to treat rejection of transplanted organs, including the heart, kidneys and liver (Ortho Biotech), DOXIL: metastatic ovarian cancer in refractory patients, AIDS-related Kaposi's sarcoma (Tibotec/ALZA), ANTIVIROGRAM HIV-1: phenotyping assay and TYPE HIV-1: predicts the virus' susceptibility to antiretroviral drugs (Virco), VELCADE: for multiple myeloma patients who've relapsed (Janssen-Ortho)

**Contraceptive:** ORTHO EVRA: first contraceptive patch (Ortho-McNeil), ORTHO TRI-CYCLEN LO, MODICON, ORTHO EVRA, ORTHO MICRONOR, ORTHO-NOVUM: all oral contraceptives (Ortho-McNeil), Evra oral contraceptives (Janssen-Ortho)

**Urology:** DITROPAN XL: overactive bladder (Ortho-McNeil/ALZA), ELMIRON relief of bladder pain or discomfort associated with interstitial cystitis (Ortho-McNeil)

## PIPELINE PRODUCTS:

For a complete updated review see: www.jnj.com/innovations/pharma_pipeline/index.htm
*   April 2006, Remicade received priority-review status by FDA for treating Crohn's disease in children; (Phase III); also in pipeline for juvenile RA, psoriasis
*   Paliperidone ER OROS: schizophrenia (Filed 11/05, other indications in Phase III
*   CNTO 1275: psoriasis (Phase III)
*   CNTO 148: rheumatoid arthritis, ankylosing spondylitis, psoriatic arthritis (Phase III)
*   ICA 17043: Sickle Cell Disease (Phase III)
*   Ceftobiprole: Complicated Skin and Skin Structure Infections, Nosocomial Pneumonia (Phase III)
*   Doripenem: Complicated UTIs, Intra Abdominal Infections, Nosocomial Pneumonia (Phase III)
*   Doxil Injections: Multiple Myeloma, Breast Cancer (Phase III)
*   Zarnestra: Acute Myeloid Leukemia
*   Yondelis: Relapsed Ovarian Cancer (Phase III)
*   Tibotec has two antiretroviral compounds in development for HIV/AIDS. TMC125 is a non-nucleoside reverse transcriptase inhibitor (NNRTI) and TMC114 is a protease inhibitor (PI). Both compounds are highly active against both wild-type and drug resistant HIV.
*   IONSYS: Acute post-operative pain (Awaiting FDA response)
*   OROS: Chronic pain (Phase III)
*   REOPRO: Percutaneous Coronary Intervention (Phase III)
*   Bay 59-7939: prevention of venous thromboembolism in hip/knee replacement surgery (Phase III)
*   Dapoxetine: premature ejaculation

# Merck & Co. Inc.

**Merck & Co. Inc.**
PO Box 100
One Merck Drive
Whitehouse Station, NJ 08889-0100
Phone: 908-423-1000
Fax: 908-735-1253
Web Site: www.merck.com

## HIGHLIGHTS:

- Slogan: "Where People Come First"
- Chairman/ CEO: Richard T. Clark
- Total Revenues 2005: $22.0 Billion
- R&D 2005: $3.8 million
- 7,800 researchers
- Sales Force Size: 8,000
- Number of Employees: 61,500
- Stock Symbol: MRK
- Ranked #95 out of Top 500 Companies in terms of revenue by *Fortune* magazine
- Ranked #3 of Top Pharmaceutical Companies by *Pharmaceutical Executive* magazine
- *Working Mother* magazine's Top 100 Best Places to Work for working mothers
- Merck & Co. has a collaboration agreement with NicOx SA to develop antihypertensive drugs using NicOx's proprietary nitric oxide-donating technology
- One of just five major pharmaceutical research companies in the world that is actively pursuing the development of new vaccines
- Co-promote Zetia and Vytorin with Schering-Plough; has partnership with AstraZeneca for Nexium
- Four of the company's products have achieved blockbuster status (sales of more than $1 billion each): Fosamax, Singular, Zocor, Cozaar/Hyzaar
- Merck had a setback starting Sept 2004 with its worldwide voluntary withdrawal of VIOXX from the market. It was one of their top blockbuster performing products, however they are working hard to change their business to reclaim a top spot in the pharmaceutical industry. Their strategy is called: *Merck's Plan to Win*

## MAJOR PRODUCTS AND THERAPEUTIC AREAS:

Merck & Co., Inc. concentrates in the discovery, development, manufacture and marketing of various products for human and animal health. The company's products consist of therapeutic and preventive agents sold by prescription for the treatment and prevention of human disorders. Vaccines are a huge part of Merck's business.

**Cardiovascular:** ZOCOR: atherosclerosis, COZAAR and HYZAAR: hypertension/heart failure, stroke risk reduction, VYTORIN: cholesterol (Merck/Schering-Plough) ZETIA: cholesterol (Merck/Schering-Plough)
**Endocrinology:** JANUVIA: medicine to treat type 2 diabetes
**Osteoporosis:** FOSAMAX: prevention of osteoporosis, FOSAMAX PLUS D: prevention of osteoporosis in once weekly pill with Vitamin D
**Respiratory:** SINGULAIR: respiratory product, asthma, seasonal allergic rhinitis
**Vaccines:** VARIVAX: live virus vaccine of chickenpox, M-M-R II: pediatric vaccine for the prevention of measles, mumps and rubella, PNEUMOVAX: vaccine for the prevention of pneumococcal disease, RECOMBIVAX HB: vaccine for the prevention of hepatitis B, ROTATEQ: vaccine for the prevention of rotavirus gastroenteritis in infants and children, VAQTA: hepatitis A vaccine for children as young as one year, PROQUAD: combination vaccine for measles, mumps, rubella and chickenpox
**Anti-Infectives:** PRIMAXIN and CANCIDAS: antibacterial/antifungal products, INVANZ: moderate to severe

complicated skin/skin structure infections, intra-abdominal infections, UTIs, CAP and pelvic infections
**Urology:** PROSCAR, symptomatic benign prostate enlargement
**Ophthalmology:** COSOPT: reduction of elevated intraocular pressure (IOP) in patients with open-angle glaucoma or ocular hypertension, TRUSOPT: opthalmological products
**Pain Management:** MAXALT: acute migraines
**Hair Loss:** PROPECIA, which is used for the treatment of male pattern hair loss
**Oncology:** EMEND: prevention of nausea/vomiting in cancer patients undergoing chemotherapy
**Virology:** CRIXIVAN: in combination with other antiretroviral agents for HIV infection, STOCRIN: HIV infection

## PIPELINE PRODUCTS:

Promising drugs in late-stage development for diabetes, insomnia, heart disease, high cholesterol and HIV/AIDS continue to advance through our pipeline
**Vaccines:** GARDASIL: vaccine for cervical cancer and the prevention of Human Papillomavirus, genital warts (at FDA for review), ZOSTAVAX: vaccine to help prevent shingles in patients over 60, received a positive review by an FDA Advisory Committee, a critical step toward expected FDA approval in 2006
**Pharmaceuticals:**
ARCOXIA: Arthritis/Pain (at FDA)
GABODAXOL: Insomnia (Phase III)
MK-0518: AIDS (Phase III)
MK-0524A, 0524B: Atherosclerosis (Phase III)
MK-0517: CINV (Phase III)
MK-0431A: Diabetes (Phase III)

For more pipeline products in Phase II and I: www.merck.com/finance/annualreport/ar2005/research_pipeline.html

# Novartis

**Novartis AG**
Lichtstrasse 35
Basel, 4056, Switzerland
Phone: 41 61 324 11 11
Fax: 41 61 324 80 01
Web Site: www.novartis.com
US Investor Relations: (212) 830-2433

## HIGHLIGHTS:

* Chairman/ CEO: Daniel L. Vasella
* Total Revenues 2005: $32.2 Billion
* R&D 2005: $4.8 Billion
* Researchers: Not available
* Sales Force Size: 6,000 U.S. pharmaceutical reps
* Number of Employees: 22,000 in US and 90,924 globally
* Stock Symbol: NVS
* Novartis was created in 1996 by the merger of the Swiss companies Ciba-Geigy and Sandoz
* In 2005, pharmaceutical sales grew by 10% ($20.3 billion)
* Novartis is the only company with leadership positions in both the patented and generic pharmaceuticals
* Ranked #7 of Top Pharmaceutical Companies in terms of sales revenue by *Pharmaceutical Executive* magazine
* According to *Business Week*, Novartis was among the 50 Best Global Brands

- In 2005, Novartis was listed among the 50 Most Respected Companies by the *Financial Times* and *Barron's* and also featured in *Fortune* magazine's list of the world's 50 Most Admired Companies
- *Working Mother* magazine's Top 100 Best Places to Work for working mothers
- Novartis has a strategic alliance with Infinity Pharmaceuticals, Inc. to discover, develop and commercialize drugs targeting Bcl-2 protein family members for the treatment of cancer indications; and collaboration with Alnylam Pharmaceuticals, Inc. to develop RNAi therapeutics for pandemic flu
- Novartis acquired the Chiron Corporation in 2006, a pharmaceutical and vaccines company
- In 2004, acquired Bristol-Myers Squibb's North American OTC division, of which Excedrin is one of the leaders in OTC analgesics

## MAJOR PRODUCTS AND THERAPEUTIC AREAS:

Novartis AG engages in the research, development, manufacture and marketing of health care products. It has three divisions: Pharmaceuticals, Sandoz and Consumer Health. The Pharmaceuticals division develops and markets pharmaceuticals in various therapeutic areas, including cardiovascular and metabolism, neuroscience, respiratory and dermatology, specialty medicines, oncology and hematology, transplantation and immunology, and ophthalmic diseases, as well as arthritis, bone, gastrointestinal, hormone replacement therapy and infectious diseases. The Sandoz division supplies generic pharmaceuticals that develops, produces and markets these drugs along with pharmaceutical and biotechnological active substances intermediates to wholesalers, pharmacies, hospitals and other healthcare outlets. It offers antibiotics, treatments for central nervous system disorders, gastrointestinal medicines, cardiovascular treatments and hormone therapies. The Consumer Health division operates five units, such as over-the-counter (OTC) self-medication products, animal health, medical nutrition, Gerber and lens and vision care. Common OTC products include: Vagistat, Ex-Lax, Maalox, Lamisil AT, Theraflu, Triaminic, Bufferin, Excedrin, Keri Lotion, Mineral Ice, No-Doz.
A fourth division is planned to be created after the complete acquisition of Chiron Corporation – Vaccines and Diagnostics.
**Cardiovascular and Metabolism:** Diovan: used in the treatment of hypertension, Diovan HCT: same, but with addition of a diuretic, Lotrel: combination product of amlodipine and benazepril hydrochloride used in the treatment of hypertension, Lescol XL: used in the treatment of atherosclerosis vascular disease to lower cholesterol, Lotensin: ACE inhibitor, antihypertensive agent, Lotensin HCT: antihypertensive agent in combo with a diuretic
**Neuroscience:** Ritalin Hydrochloride/Ritalin LA/Ritalin SR: for a stabilizing effect in ADHD/ADD, Trileptal: used in the treatment of epilepsy, Anafranil: tricyclic antidepressant, Leponex: used in the treatment of schizophrenia, Comtan/Stalevo: used in the treatment of Parkinson's Disease, Entumin: neuroleptic agent used in the treatment of schizophrenia, Exelon: used in the treatment of dementia of Alzheimer's Disease, Focalin: part of total treatment program to stabilize ADHD/ADD, Tegretol XR: used as an anticonvulsant drug
**Respiratory:** Foradil Aerolizer: used in the treatment of asthma and in the prevention of bronchospasm, Xolair: used in the treatment of asthma
**Dermatology:** Denavir: used in the treatment of recurrent herpes labialis (cold sores), Elidel: used in the treatment of eczema
**Endocrine/Diabetes:** Anturan: long-term treatment of gout, Starlix: used in monotherapy to lower blood glucose in patients with Type II diabetes
**Oncology and Hematology:** Gleevec: used in the treatment of Chronic Myeloid Leukemia and Gastrointestinal Stromal Tumors, Zometa: used in the treatment of bone metastasis in a variety of tumor types, Sandostatin LAR Depot: used to reduce blood levels of growth hormone and IGF-I in acromegaly patients at the tumor site, Femara: used in the treatment of advanced or metastatic breast cancer, Navoban: used in the treatment of cancer chemotherapy-induced nausea and vomiting
**Transplantation and immunology:** Neoral/Sandimmun/Simulect: immunosuppressive agents for transplantations
**Ophthalmic diseases:** Angiscein: for ophthalmic angiography and angioscopy, Apresoline: periferal vasodilator, Miochol-E: used to obtain miosis (contraction of the pupil) in seconds after delivery of the lens in cataract surgery and other eye surgeries where rapid miosis is required, Voltaren Ophthalmic: used for the treatment of postoperative inflammation following cataract surgery and for the temporary relief of pain and sensitivity to light following corneal refractive surgery, Zaditor: used for the temporary prevention of itching of the eye due to allergies, Rescula: used for treatment of ocular hypertension and

mild to moderate glaucoma, Spersallerg: soothes irritated eyes from allergies, Sulf-10 Dropperette: used in treatment of conjunctivitis and other superficial ocular infections due to susceptible microorganisms, Visudyne: used in the treatment of age-related macular degeneration and any disease associated with rapidly growing tissue

**Arthritis/Bone:** Voltaren: nonsteroidalanti-inflammatory, antirheumatic agent, Aredia: inhibitor of cancer-related bone loss, Cataflam: used in the treatment of the signs and symptoms of osteoarthritis and rheumatoid arthritis, Cibacalcin: used in the treatment of Paget's disease of bone and osteoporosis, Miacalcin: used in the treatment of postmenopausal osteoporosis, Voltaren XR: used as a treatment of the symptoms of osteoarthritis and rheumatoid arthritis

**Gastrointestinal:** Enablex: used as a once daily dose for the effective treatment of overactive bladder, Zelnorm: used in the treatment of Irritable Bowel Syndrome

**Hormone replacement therapy:** Combipatch/Estraderm/Vivelle Dot: each is used in the treatment of vasomotor symptoms associated with menopause

**Infectious diseases:** Lamisil: antifungal agent, Riamet: used in the treatment of malaria, Famvir: used in the treatment of recurrent genital herpes and shingles, Lamprene: used in treatment of leprosy

## PIPELINE PRODUCTS:

Novartis has a total of 75 development projects in their pipeline, of which 52 are in phases II and III or in registration. Two of Novartis' key growth areas of development for the future are oncology and cardiovascular diseases. For more information: www.novartis.com/about_novartis/en/product_pipeline.shtml

- Exjade given approval in 2005 for iron overload due to frequent blood transfusions
- Glivec submitted to FDA for approval as treatment for four rare types of cancer
- FTY720: multiple sclerosis (Phase II)
- Galvus, an oral therapy for type 2 diabetes, a new drug application was accepted for review by FDA in March 2006
- LAF237: diabetes
- Lucentis: AMD
- Rasilez, SPP100: for hypertension, first in a new antihypertensive class called renin inhibitors
- QAB149: asthma, COPD
- LIC477: bipolar disorder
- PTK787: colorectal cancer
- Valopicitabine (NM283), a treatment for hepatitis C
- Femara: breast cancer

# Pfizer Inc

**Pfizer Inc**
235 East 42nd Street
New York, NY 10017
Phone: 212-573-2323
Fax: 212-573-7851
Web Site: www.pfizer.com

## HIGHLIGHTS:

- Chairman/ CEO: Jeffrey B. Kindler
- Total Revenues 2005: $51.3 Billion
- R&D 2005: $7.4 Billion (Pfizer boasts the industry's largest pharmaceutical R&D organization)
- One of the top R&D companies over all industries-up there with GM and IBM
- 12,000 researchers

- Sales Force Size: 8,800
- Number of Employees: 106,000
- Stock Symbol: PFE
- Ranked #31 out of Top 500 Companies in terms of revenue by *Fortune* magazine
- Ranked #1 of Top Pharmaceutical Companies by *Pharmaceutical Executive* magazine
- *Fortune* magazine's 100 Best Companies to work for in 2000 (ranked 20th overall, highest among all pharmaceutical companies)
- Eight of the company's products have achieved blockbuster status (sales of more than $1 billion each)
- *Working Mother* magazine's Top 10 Best Places to Work for working mothers
- *Industry Week* magazine's Top 100 Best Managed Companies
- Co-promote products with Eisai Inc., OSI Pharmaceuticals, Inc, Serono, Inc, and Boehringer Ingelheim Corporation
- Acquired and successfully merged with Warner-Lambert (2000) and Pharmacia (2003) to create the world's fastest-growing major pharmaceutical company and is the world's largest company devoted to healthcare
- Taking a huge step in America by introducing a program to more than 40 million uninsured Americans to get Pfizer pharmaceuticals for free or at significant discount
- *Advertising Age* 2001 Marketer of the Year Award
- Had goal to file 20 major new medicines in the US in the 5 year period ending in 2006; now believe 19 will be approved
- Acquired Vicuron (Anti-infectives Company) in 2005
- Sold its Consumer Healthcare division to Johnson & Johnson in 2006

## MAJOR PRODUCTS AND THERAPEUTIC AREAS:

Pfizer has two segments: Human Health and Animal Health. The Human Health segment offers treatments for cardiovascular and metabolic diseases, central nervous system disorders, arthritis and pain, infectious and respiratory diseases, urogenital conditions, cancer, eye disease, endocrine disorders and allergies.

**Anti-Infectives:** Zithromax®/ZmaxTM antibiotic, Unasyn® injectable antibacterial, Vfend® antifungal, Vibramycin® antibiotic

**Metabolic/Diabetes:** Exubera® insulin Inhalation Powder (approved Jan 2006), Genotropin® human growth hormone, Glucotrol®/Glucotrol XL® Type 2 Diabetes, hyperglycemia

**Neuroscience and Pain Management:** Lyrica® neuropathic/nerve pain, Aricept® alzheimers (Eisai Inc), Celebrex® arthritis pain, pain, Zoloft® depression, anxiety, Dilantin® anti-epileptic drug, Geodon® acute mania, bipolar mixed episodes, schizophrenia Neurontin® nerve pain, partial seizures, Rebif® multiple sclerosis (Serono, Inc), Relpax® migraines Xanax®/Xanax XR® panic disorders, Zarontin® anti-convulsant

**Cardiovascular:** Lipitor® cholesterol, Norvasc® hypertension, Accupril®/Accuretic® hypertension Caduet® hypertension and cholesterol, Cardura® hypertension by lowering blood pressure benign prostatic hyperplasia (BPH), Procardia®/Procardia XL® anti-anginal drug, hypertension

**Oncology:** Sutent® advanced renal cell carcinoma and gastrointestinal stromal tumor

**Urology:** Viagra® men's health, Cardura® benign prostatic hyperplasia (BPH), Detrol® LA overactive bladder

**Virology:** Viracept® HIV

**Allergy/Respiratory:** Zyrtec® allergies, Spiriva® HandiHaler® COPD (Boehringer Ingelheim)

**Ocular:** Xalatan® open angle glaucoma, ocular hypertension, Macugen® age-related macular degeneration (OSI Pharmaceuticals)

## PIPELINE PRODUCTS:

More than 130 potential products in their R&D pipeline:
- Torcetrapib/atorvastatin: combo product for cholesterol-Phase III

- Zeven: Anti-Infective
- PF-04136307: RA/Diabetes
- VR-1 Antagonist: Pain
- PF-3491390: Liver Disease
- PF3512676: Oncology
- T2-TrpRS: Macular Degenration
- Syk tyrosine kinase inhibitor: Allergic Asthma
- UK-427,857: first-in-class CCR-5 inhibitor for treatment of HIV disease
- Indiplon: insomnia
- Parecoxib: injectable for acute pain
- Edotecarin: colorectal cancer and glioma
- Varenicline: smoking cessation
- Asenapine: schizophrenia, bipolar disorder
- Zithromax-chloroquine: malaria

# Schering-Plough Corp.

**Schering-Plough Corp.**
2000 Galloping Hill Road
Kenilworth, NJ 07033
Phone: 908-298-4000
Fax: 908-298-7082
Web Site: www.schering-plough.com

## HIGHLIGHTS:

- Chairman/ CEO: Fred Hassan
- Total Revenues 2005: $9.5 Billion
- R&D 2005: $1.9 Billion
- Researchers: Not available
- Sales Force Size: 4,500 U.S. based representatives
- Number of Employees: 32,600
- Stock Symbol: SGP
- Ranked #250 out of Top 500 Companies in terms of revenue by *Fortune* magazine
- Ranked #17 of Top Pharmaceutical Companies based on sales revenue by *Pharmaceutical Executive* magazine
- *Working Mother* magazine's Top 10 Best Places to Work for working mothers
- Co-promotes with Bayer (Avelox/Cipro) and Merck (Vytorin is Merck's and Zetia is Schering Plough's and the combination pill achieved $2.4 billion 2005 sales)
- Collaborates with Pharmacopeia on the discovery of new compounds. In April 2006, Schering-Plough chose another of the Pharmacopeia's compounds for further development as a potential treatment for respiratory disease
- Collaborates with Sankyo Company Ltd for olmesartan (hypertension) in Latin America; Centocor, Inc. (a Johnson and Johnson company) for Remicade and Phase III Golimumab; and PTC Therapeutics, Inc. for the development of preclinical compounds for the oral treatment of hepatitis C virus infection and other viral diseases
- Acquired Neo Genesis Pharmaceuticals Inc, in 2005, a privately held biopharmaceutical company focused on the discovery of small molecule drugs
- In 2003, their new CEO initiated a five phase plan, the Action Agenda, to help bring company back to top of the sector. In 2005, six of their top 10 products achieved double digit growth (not including Zetia and Vytorin)

**MAJOR PRODUCTS AND THERAPEUTIC AREAS:**

Schering-Plough Corporation engages in the discovery, development, manufacture and marketing of drug therapies. It has three segments: Prescription Pharmaceuticals, Consumer Health Care and Animal Health. The Prescription Pharmaceuticals segment offers primary care products, like allergy/respiratory products, antibiotics for certain respiratory and skin infections and dermatologicals, including steroid creams, lotions and ointments; specialty care products, such as anti-virals, anti-inflammatories, oncology drugs, acute coronary care products and products for other disorders; and cholesterol-absorption inhibitors and cholesterol-lowering tablets. This segment sells its products to hospitals, certain managed care organizations, wholesale distributors and retail pharmacists. The Consumer Health Care segment offers non-drowsy antihistamines; cold and allergy, allergy sinus, flu and nasal decongestant tablets; nasal decongestant sprays and laxative tablets; and foot care (Dr. Scholl's) and sun care products (BAIN DE SOLEIL and Coppertone). The Animal Health segment offers steroids for otitis in dogs, topical insecticide for dogs, pet recovery services, anti-inflammatory/analgesic for dogs, parasiticide for sea lice in salmon, antibiotic for farm-raised fish and bovine and swine antibiotics, anti-inflammatory, pneumonia vaccines. This segment sells its products to veterinarians, distributors and animal producers.

**Allergy/Respiratory:** CLARINEX: for allergy symptoms caused by seasonal allergens such as ragweed, grass, tree pollens and year-round allergens such as dust mites, animal dander and mold spores, ASMANEX TWISTHALER: asthma for patients 12 years and older, FORADIL AEROLIZER: management of Chronic Obstructive Pulmonary Disease (COPD) and Asthma Relief, NASONEX: night and day relief for congestion and other indoor and outdoor nasal allergy symptoms, PROVENTIL INHALATION SOLUTION: relief of bronchospasm in patients 12 years and older with reversible obstructive airway disease and acute attacks of bronchospasm, PROVENTIL HFA INHALATION AEROSOL: for the treatment and prevention of bronchospasm in patients 4 years and older with reversible obstructive airway disease and for the prevention of exercise-induced bronchospasm
**Antibiotics:** Avelox: a broad-spectrum fluoroquinolone antibacterial for respiratory tract infections (RTIs) in adults 18 years of age and older, including: Acute Bacterial Sinusitis (ABS), Acute Bacterial Exacerbation of Chronic Bronchitis (ABECB), Skin and Skin Structure Infections and Community-Acquired Pneumonia (CAP), (Co-promoted with Bayer) CIPRO: broad spectrum fluoroquinolone for urinary tract infections (UTIs) such as acute uncomplicated cystitis, pyelonephritis and chronic bacterial prostatitis (Co-promoted with Bayer)
**Dermatology:** LOTRIMIN: Topical anti-fungal for athlete's feet and jock itch, TINACTIN: topical anti-fungal for athlete's feet, jock itch, ringworm and infections on scalp and nails, DIPROLENE GEL/LOTION: for the relief of inflammatory and pruritic manifestations of corticosteroid-responsive dermatoses, ELOCON CREAM/LOTION/ OINTMENT: corticosteroid for the relief of inflammatory and pruritic manifestations of corticosteroid-responsive dermatoses, LOTRISONE CREAM/LOTION: topical corticosteroid for symptomatic inflammatory tenia pedis, tenia cruris and tinea corporis
**Anti-Virals:** PEG-INTRON INJECTION: a chronic hepatitis C treatment, PEG-INTRON REDIPEN: first and only pen delivery system for administering pegylated interferon therapy for chronic hepatitis C, REBETOL: indicated for use in combination with PEG-INTRON INJECTION and with INTRON A INJECTION for the treatment of chronic hepatitis C virus in patients at least 18 years of age with compensated liver disease previously untreated with interferon alpha
**Arthritis/Immunology:** Remicade: a biologic treatment for ulcerative colitis, Crohn's Disease, rheumatoid arthritis, ankylosing spondylitis, or psoriatic arthritis
**Cardiology:** VYTORIN: combination medication (Zocor plus Zetia) for lowering cholesterol, ZETIA: blocks the absorption of cholesterol that comes from food, INTEGRILIN INJECTION: prevent occlusion of the arteries to help reduce the incidence of heart attack in patients with acute coronary syndrome (ACS) (unstable angina/non-ST-segment myocardial infarction) and those undergoing percutaneous coronary intervention (PCI), also for the treatment of patients at time of PCI, including in patients undergoing intracoronary stenting, K-DUR: for patients with hypokalemia, in digitalis intoxication, or with cardiac arrhythmias and with hypokalemic familial periodic paralysis, NITRO-DUR: transdermal infusion for the prevention of angina pectoris due to coronary artery disease
**Oncology:** INTRON A INJECTION: for treatment of malignant melanoma, hairy cell leukemia, chronic hepatitis B, chronic hepatitis C, condylomata acuminata, follicular (non-Hodgkin's) lymphoma and AIDS-related Kaposi's sarcoma, TEMODAR: for the treatment of adult patients with newly diagnosed glioblastoma multiforme concomitantly with radiotherapy and then as maintenance treatment, and for

the treatment of adult patients with refractory anaplastic astrocytoma
**Urology:** LEVITRA: erectile dysfunction

## PIPELINE PRODUCTS:

Filed w/ FDA: Garenoxacin: antibiotic, Noxafil: fungal infections
*   Phase III: Golimumab CNTO 148: Inflammatory Disease, Sarasar: malignant melanoma, Suboxone: opiate addiction, Temodar: metastatic melanoma, Vytorin: other indications based on recent outcomes trials
*   Phase II: Vicriviroc: HIV, Protease Inhibitor: Hepatitis C, PDE 5: Eerectile Dysfunction, Adenosine 2a Receptor Antagonist: Parkinson's Disease

# Wyeth

**Wyeth**
Five Giralda Farms
Madison, NJ 07940
Phone: 973-660-5000
Fax: 973-660-5771
Web Site: www.wyeth.com

## HIGHLIGHTS:

*   Chairman/ CEO: Robert A. Essner
*   Total Revenues 2005: $18.8 Billion
*   R&D 2005:  $2.7 Billion
*   6,000 researchers
*   Sales Force Size: 4,450
*   Number of Employees: 52,000
*   Stock Symbol: WYE
*   Formerly known as American Home Products Corporation and changed its name to Wyeth in 2002
*   Ranked #119 out of Top 500 Companies by revenues by *Fortune* magazine
*   Ranked #9 of Top Pharmaceutical Companies by *Pharmaceutical Executive* magazine
*   *Working Mother* magazine's Top 100 Best Places to work for eighth consecutive year
*   Five of the company's products have achieved blockbuster status (sales of more than $1 billion each): Effexor XR®, Protonix®, Enbrel®, Premarin®, Prevnar®
*   In 2005, received honors for "Best Management Team" and "Best Partnership Alliance" by Scrip, an International Pharmaceutical Business Publication
*   *Science* magazine in 2005 named Wyeth Pharmaceuticals among its Top 20 Biotech and Pharmaceutical Employers
*   Awarded the prestigious Discoverers Award from the Pharmaceutical Research and Manufacturers of America (PhRMA) in 2005 for the development of Prevnar®; the award goes to scientists whose research and development efforts have greatly benefited humankind and whose dedication and interest in improving the quality of life exemplify the best in the research-based pharmaceutical industry
*   Co-promotes products with King Pharmaceuticals and Amgen
*   Has collaborations with Progenics Pharmaceuticals, Inc. and Trubion Pharmaceuticals, Inc.

## MAJOR PRODUCTS AND THERAPEUTIC AREAS:

Wyeth is divided into three segments: Pharmaceuticals, Consumer Health Care Products and Animal Health Care Products. Its Pharmaceuticals segment offers neuroscience therapies, cardiovascular products, nutrition products, gastroenterology drugs, anti-infectives, oncology therapies, musculoskeletal therapies, hemophilia treatments, immunological products and women's health care products. Its Consumer Healthcare segment sells over-the-counter health care products, such as analgesics; cough/cold/allergy remedies; nutritional supplements; and hemorrhoidal, asthma and personal care items. Commonly known consumer products: Centrum, Advil, Robitussin, Chap Stick, Dimetapp, Fiber Con, Preparation H, Caltrate, Anbesol.

**Anti-Infectives/Infectious Diseases:** Tygacil®: IV antibiotic for complicated skin and skin structure infections and complicated intra-abdominal infections, Zosyn®: IV treatment for moderate to severe infections caused by piperacillin-resistant, piperacillin/tazobactam-susceptible strains of indicated organisms

**Neuroscience:** Effexor XR®/Effexor®: depression, generalized anxiety disorder (GAD), or social anxiety disorder

**Cardiovascular:** ALTACE®: hypertension, reduction of cardiovascular risk in high-risk patients aged 55+ (co-promote with King Pharmaceuticals), Cordarone® I.V.: treatment and prophylaxis of frequently recurring ventricular fibrillation and hemodynamically unstable ventricular tachycardia

**Oncology:** Mylotarg® IV: myeloid leukemia for adults 60+ in first relapse, Neumega®: prevention of severe thrombocytopenia and the reduction of the need for platelet transfusions following myelosuppressive chemotherapy in adult patients

**Gastroenterology:** Protonix®: gastroesophageal reflux disease, nighttime heartburn

**Musculoskeletal:** Enbrel®: rheumatoid arthritis (co-promote with Amgen)

**Hemophilia:** (Hemophilia is an inherited disease that prevents the blood from clotting properly) BeneFIX®: control and prevention of hemorrhagic episodes in patients with hemophilia B (congenital factor IX deficiency or Christmas disease), including control and prevention of bleeding in surgical settings, ReFacto®: control and prevention of hemorrhagic episodes and for surgical prophylaxis and for short-term routine prophylaxis to reduce the frequency of spontaneous bleeding episodes in patients with hemophilia A

**Immunological:** Rapamune: prophylaxis of organ rejection in patients aged 13+ receiving renal transplants

**Women's Healthcare:** Premarin: used after menopause to reduce moderate to severe hot flashes; to treat moderate to severe dryness, itching and burning, in and around the vagina; and to help reduce osteoporosis (thin weak bones), PREMPRO™: used after menopause in women with a uterus to reduce moderate to severe hot flashes; to treat moderate to severe dryness, itching and burning, in and around the vagina; and to help reduce osteoporosis, Alesse: oral contraceptive, PREMPHASE®: same as PREMPRO but with 2 pills per 15 day period and each has different levels of estrogen

**Vaccines:** HibTITER® Haemophilus b Conjugate Vaccine: immunization of children ages 2-71 months against invasive disease caused by H. influenza type B, Prevnar® Pneumococcal 7-Valent Conjugate Vaccine: immunization of children and toddlers against invasive diseases caused by 6 serotypes of S. pneumonia

**Other:** Phenergan: Motion sickness/nausea

## PIPELINE PRODUCTS:

Wyeth is exploring more than 60 new therapies for medical conditions such as diabetes, breast cancer, multiple sclerosis, HIV, Alzheimer's disease and schizophrenia.

- DVS-233: Depression, vasomotor symptoms (Phase III)
- CCI-779: Breast Cancer, renal cell cancer, mantle cell lymphoma (Phase III)
- Protonix Oral Pediatric (Phase III)
- Tygacil (Phase III)
- Bazedoxifene (Phase III)
- Bifprunox (Phase III)
- Effexor: panic indication (Phase III)

# ACKNOWLEDGMENTS

Before I thank the many people without whom I could not have written this book, I must first begin with the members of my family who have always been there for me and cheered me on. They inspire me to be a better person in more ways than they will ever realize.

I am tremendously fortunate that the man who has been my best friend since middle school is an industry veteran. Lou went out of his way to respond to each and every one of my questions, big or small, during the writing of the book. He read through every draft of the manuscript, providing invaluable advice and feedback. He has been as genuinely interested in the overall progress in the book as he always has been in my well-being.

At Tom Ruff Company, I have the honor of working with some of the most talented, dedicated and professional individuals I've ever known. Their hard work enabled me to take a year-long sabbatical to live in New York and write this book. Anytime I needed anything, they came through. Like Lou, they all read the manuscript and provided feedback. I am tremendously proud to work with them every day.

Of my team members, Shari Lee Douglas deserves particular mention. While I was in New York, she was the glue that held everyone together. Her expert contributions to the company and feedback on the book were absolutely essential. Equally important, if not more so, are her integrity, faith and big heart. Her many hugs and great enthusiasm for this project were more important than I can say.

Andi Atteberry became my personal assistant just as the book was near completion — but what a life changer she has been. Anything I pass off to her is handled immediately, impeccably and without complaint. Her ability to take so many things off my plate gives me the ability to focus on what's most important in my life. Her calm unflappability is priceless.

Without Eric Schade I might not have undertaken this book at all. Eric sat down with me one day at The Coffee Shop on Union Square several years ago and encouraged me to move to New York and fulfill my dream of undertaking this challenge. I made the life-changing decision then and there. Throughout, his feedback was invaluable. He is a gifted, highly intelligent writer. On all the days when I felt shut down by writer's block, Eric showed me how to push on through. He believed in me and in my writing ability before I did.

I met John Pollack at Jack's Coffee Shop on West Tenth Street near my New York home and he and I have become great friends. An accomplished writer, he became a tremendous resource for me in the writing of this book. He took the time out of a hectic schedule to do line edits for the entire book and to share his feedback at important junctures in its writing. He was more of a help than he will ever realize.

I am fortunate to have had a tremendous resource in my friend Brett Butler, who is one of the best salesmen I know. With thoughtfulness and great attention to detail, he read the book and provided invaluable help on everything in it that relates to the art of selling.

My friend Jennifer Abram provided crucial insights from where she once sat in the corporate world. I am honored to have helped her secure her first job in the industry and to have watched her career unfold. I have great respect for her and the recruiting work she did on the corporate side.

My childhood friend Jonathan Siade-Cox is a veteran of the industry who invested precious time to review the earliest drafts of the book. He commands my respect as a friend and for his conduct in the business world.

Another old friend, this one dating back to high school, is Robbie Evans, who acted as an invaluable resource to me. I also want to thank him for his great integrity as a person and for his long friendship.

Keri Oberg is both a special friend and a special human being. The passion and integrity with which she pursues her career is inspiring to me and to so many others. She continues to grow professionally, while always keeping intact her native compassion and deep sense of the value and preciousness of life.

For the past 15 years, I've seen my writing mentor and great friend Boots LeBaron (yes, that is his real name) almost daily at our local coffee shop in Manhattan Beach. A former childhood actor and newspaper writer who later ran his own public relations firm (you probably recognize his phrase, "Give a hoot. Don't pollute"), Boots always shares wonderful stories with me, brings me articles to read and encourages my writing. Above all, I value his insights on life.

Paul Cox, my trusted friend and spiritual mentor, is someone who is always there for me and who I highly esteem. I thank him for his feedback while the book was in its final stages.

My friend Heidi-Anne Mooney did yeoman's work for me, researching and providing us with important feedback about aspects of the interview process — all this during the final stages of her second pregnancy.

Zoe Korstvedt created the look of the book and of our company website. Her instincts are genius and I rely implicitly on her guidance. Timothy Brittain meticulously and stylishly laid out the book page-by-page and then faithfully saw it through countless revisions. I thank him and David S. Cohen, who provided expert proofing. Thanks are also due to Bill Frank, who regularly shared his important insights into the book publishing industry.

I began working with Kerry Gladden near the book's completion and have quickly come to trust and look to her opinion.

I am honored that Ann Marsh decided to take on my project and can't imagine having done it without her. Ann took virtually everything I wrote, tore it apart, edited, organized and massaged it — optimistic and encouraging throughout — and then put it all back together again. I deeply appreciate the many hard hours she spent transforming this book from rough draft to reality. I thank her for her guidance, counsel, encouragement, compassion, integrity and — most important — her friendship.

So many other people took time out of very busy schedules to help me reflect on the important issues in this field and to lend me their expertise. For this, I thank Angela Michell, Dr. David Clayton, John Clayton, Alex Jonas, Alexandra Olympios and Kathryn L. Tomasewski. For their unfailing support before and during the book's production, I thank Bob and Melinda Blanchard, Keith Borgschatz, Kelly Buffington, Kelly Connery, Jenny Hellman, Rachel Isenberg, Garrick Sakado and Grace Wang. Thanks go, too, to the 150 working sales representatives and 20 district managers who took the time to participate in my survey, and to Rebecca Fisher and Frank Pichel who helped set those surveys up.

I offer my thanks, as well, to so many others who must go unnamed, whose counsel, input, guidance and friendship over the years have meant more than I can say.

# GLOSSARY

**Behavioral interviewing** — A technique in which the interviewer asks specific questions about real-life situations designed to evaluate a prospective employee's ability to analyze, respond to and learn from his or her experience. (Chap. 10)

**B.I.D.** — In prescriptions, abbreviation from the Latin for "twice a day." (Chap. 5)

**Brag book** — A professional-looking three-ring binder containing from 15 to 20 pages of materials: diplomas, letters of recommendation, awards, proof of sales rankings and other items that document your accomplishments for prospective employers. (Chap. 2)

**Close, the** — The art of completing the transaction at the end of a sales call. (Chap.13)

**Creative follow-up** — Clever, often amusing ways to thank an interviewer for a positive interview experience that reinforce your desire for the job and your salesmanship and style. (Chap. 12)

**Detail** — Industry name for a pharmaceutical sales call. (Chap. 8)

**Field preceptorship** — (Chap. 4) *See* **ride-along.**

**Field ride** — (Chap. 4) *See* **ride-along.**

**Headhunter** — A professional who finds corporate employment for jobseekers. Formally called *recruiter*. (Intro)

**Knockout factor** — An element on one's job application that is grounds for automatic disqualification, e.g., a criminal conviction. (Chap. 1)

**Managed care status** — A drug's managed care status indicates whether or not and how a medication is covered by various insurance programs. (Chap. 5)

**Me-too drug** — A medication similar to others on the market. (Chap. 8)

**Metabolized** — Subjected to the biochemical processes by which the body assimilates and makes use of medication. (Chap. 5)

**Panel interview** — An interview conducted by a group of interviewers. (Chap. 11)

**PhRMA** — The nonprofit Pharmaceutical Research and Manufacturer's of America, which represents the country's leading pharmaceutical research and biotechnology companies. (Chap. 1)

**Pharmaceutical representative association** — An organization for the benefit of all pharmaceutical sales representatives in a given locality where day-to-day market realities are discussed anonymously and with candor. (Chap. 5)

**Ride-along** — A day in the field with a working pharmaceutical sales representative, sometimes set up by the company as part of the interview process so that both the jobseeker and the company can get an extended, realistic look at one another. Also called field preceptorship or field ride. (Chap. 7)

**STAR format** — In behavioral interview questions, a method of answering that incorporates Situation, Task, Action and Result: describe the *situation*, outline the *task* you faced in dealing with it, relate the *actions* you took to accomplish this task and explain the *result* that ensued. (Chap. 10)

Pharmaceutical Representative Associations

Tom Ruff's List of Recommended
Sales and Motivational Books

# Pharmaceutical Representative Associations

*Pharmaceutical Representative* magazine's national directory of professional sales representative associations is subject to change. Please check www.pharmrep.com for updates.

### ALASKA:

Alaska Pharmaceutical Representative Association
P.O. Box 771753
Eagle River, AK 99577-1753
Sue Brosnahan, president (GSK) and Nicole Boss,
vice president (Novartis)
Phone: (907) 689-7736
Fax: (907) 689-7802
E-mail: alaskapharmaceuticalreps@hotmail.com

### ARIZONA:

Arizona Medical Representative Association
Tucson, AZ
John Flores, president
Phone: (520) 370-6679
E-mail: AZMRA@representative.com

### CALIFORNIA:

Central Valley Pharmaceutical Representative
Association
Fresno, CA
Luci Azevedo
Phone: (559) 323-6454
E-mail: frankazevedo@sbcglobal.net

Medical Service Society of San Diego
P.O. Box 81866
San Diego, CA 92138
Tom Spetter, president
www.medicalservicesociety.org

Pharmaceutical Representatives of Stanislaus
County
Andria Hernandez, president (AstraZeneca)
Phone: (209) 669-8301, (209) 988-7494 or Mike
Isola
Phone: (209) 669-8301
E-mail: reps@pros-c.net
www.pros-c.net

SCPC (South Coast Pharmaceutical Committee)
(only for reps working as HIV specialists)
Orange Co., Long Beach and Palm Springs
Kimberly Murdock
E-mail: kimberly.murdock@abbott.com

### FLORIDA:

North Central Florida Medical Sales Association
107 N.E. 51st Ave.
Ocala, FL 34470
Phone: (352) 425-4345
Fax: (352) 624-0971
E-mail: thomas.goins02@pfizer.com

SFPPA (South Florida Professional Pharmaceutical Association)
Miami-Dade, Broward, Palm Beach counties
E-mail: info@sfppa.org
www.sfppa.org

### GEORGIA:

Atlanta Medical & Pharmaceutical
Representatives' Association
Pam Bailey Marinko, adviser
1828 Pembroke Jones Drive
Wilmington, NC 28405
pam.marinko@proficientlearning.com

### HAWAII:

MSRH (Medical Service Representatives of
Hawaii)
Ferdie Echiverri
Phone: (800) 662-4543 ext. 58296
E-mail: sneaky@hawaii.rr.com
www.msrh.net

### ILLINOIS:

NIMRA (Northern Illinois Medical Representative
Association - Rockford)
Karla Clark, president
Phone: (815) 979-7874

### KANSAS:

Topeka Pharmaceutical Representatives' Association
2787 S.W. Plass St.
Topeka, KS 66111
Tava Weidenbaker, president
E-mail: tavaweidenbaker@aol.com

## KENTUCKY:

Greater Louisville Pharmaceutical Representative Association
Frank S. Schramko (Ortho-McNeil division of Johnson and Johnson)
Phone: (888) 323-6700 ext. 2686
E-mail: fschramk@ibius.jnj.com

Professional Representative Organization of Northern Kentucky
Jeff Overmann
Phone: (859) 344-1935
E-mail: NKYPRO@yahoo.com

## MICHIGAN:

Metro Detroit Pharmaceutical Representatives Assoc.
49252 Paloma Dr.
Belleville, MI 48111
Shannon Ostby, president (810) 287-1499
E-mail: sostby0427@aol.com

Michigan Pharmaceutical Representative Society
815 N. Washington Ave.
Lansing, MI 48906
Mary Ianni, chairwoman
Phone: (517) 484-1466

Washtenaw Area Pharmaceutical Representative Association
P.O. Box 3151
Ann Arbor, MI 48106
www.wapra.org

Western Michigan Pharmaceutical Representative Society
Carolyn O'Grady
Phone: (616) 262-8861
E-mail: wmprs@yahoo.com

## MINNESOTA:

Arrowhead Pharmaceutical Representative Association (APRA)
Duluth, MN
John Perry
E-mail: apra_email@yahoo.com
www.arrowheadpharma.com

Twin Cities Pharmaceutical Representative Association
1360 University Ave. W., #130
St. Paul, MN 55104
Phone: (651) 690-2485
www.tcpra.com

## NEW YORK:

Pharmaceutical Representative Society of New York
Anthony DeMeis, co-founder
(201) 679-0519
anthony@pharmaceuticalrepsociety.com
Yao-Hui Huang, co-founder
(201) 941-4069
yao@pharmaceuticalrepsociety.com
www.pharmaceuticalrepsociety.com

## OKLAHOMA:

Tulsa Pharmaceutical Representative Association
Mail Boxes Etc.
Attn: TPRA
10026-A S. Mingo
Tulsa, OK 74133
Jennifer Scott, president
Eric Davies, vice president

## ONTARIO:

RAPTOR (Representative Association for Pharmaceuticals in Toronto)
214 Gowan Ave.
Toronto, ON M4J 2K6
Canada
Shane Blanchard
Email: blanch4@rogers.com

## PENNSYLVANIA:

Philadelphia Area Pharmaceutical Representative Association
Jeff McGeary, president
Phone: (215) 482-9339
Email: phillyrepassn@yahoo.com

## TEXAS:

Amarillo Pharmaceutical Representatives Association
Amy Duncan, secretary
Email: amy.duncan@spcorp.com

## WISCONSIN:

CWPRA (Central Wisconsin Pharmaceutical Representatives Association)
www.cwpra.com

# Tom Ruff's List of Recommended Sales and Motivational Books

## Sales:

1.) *The Greatest Salesman In The World* (Mandino,Og: Frederick Fell, Inc, 1968.)
2.) *Spin Selling* (Rackham, Neil: McGraw-Hill, Inc., 1988.)
3.) *Conceptual Selling* (Hieman, Stephen E. and Miller, Robert B.: Warner Books, reprint edition, 1989.)
4.) *If You're Not Out Selling, You're Being Outsold* (St. Lawrence, Michael and Johnson, Steve: Wiley, 1997.)
5.) *The Sales Bible* (Gitomer, Jeffrey H.: William Morrow, 1994.)
6.) *How to Become a Rainmaker* (Fox, Jeffrey J.: Hyperion, 2000.)
7.) *Swim With The Sharks Without Being Eaten Alive* (Mackay, Harvey: William Morrow, 1988.)

## Motivation — Life:

1.) *How to Win Friends & Influence People* (Carnegie, Dale: Simon & Schuster, 1936.)
2.) *The Power of Positive Thinking* (Peale, Norman Vincent: Prentice Hall, 1954.)
3.) *Think & Grow Rich* (Hill, Napoleon: Napoleon Hill Foundation, 1936.)
4.) *Awaken the Giant Within* (Robbins, Anthony: Simon & Schuster, 1991.)
5.) *As a Man Thinketh* (1908) (Allen, James: Book Jungle, 2006.)
6.) *Man's Search for Meaning* (Frankl, Victor: Beacon Press: 1959.)
7.) *Benjamin Franklin: An American Life* (Issacson, Walter: Simon & Schuster, 2004)
8.) *Maximum Achievement* (Tracy, Brian: Simon & Schuster, 1993.)
9.) *The Richest Man in Babylon* (Clason, George: Hawthorn, 1955.)
10.) *Rhinoceros Success* (Alexander, Scott: Rhinos Press, 1983.)
11.) *The Magic of Thinking Big* (Schwartz, David J.: Prentice Hall, 1962.)
12.) *Learned Optimism — How to Change Your Mind and Your Life* (Seligman, Martin E.P., Ph.D.: Knopf, 1990.)
13.) *The Seven Habits of Highly Effective People* (Covey, Stephen: Free Press, 1989.)

# INDEX

# NOTES

# NOTES

# NOTES

# NOTES

# NOTES

# NOTES

# NOTES

# About the Author

Tom Ruff, President and CEO of Tom Ruff Company, has placed nearly 3,000 pharmaceutical and medical sales representatives with the help of his team at Tom Ruff Company, a firm he founded nearly 16 years ago at age 24. Tom Ruff Company now services more than 100 of the nation's top pharmaceutical and medical device companies nationwide, including Johnson & Johnson, Pfizer and Abbott Laboratories.

His authoritative workbook *How to Break Into Pharmaceutical Sales: A Headhunter's Strategy* has been hailed by critics and medical industry insiders as the book to consult for pursuing a career in pharmaceutical sales. Acknowledged as a 'Best Books Award' finalist by *USA Book News*, Ruff's work has also attracted the attention of a number of online, print and broadcast media outlets including *Forbes.com, Fortune.com, Yahoo! Finance, LATimes.com, Kipplinger's.com, DallasMorningNews.com, South Bend Tribune, Easy Reader, The Beach Reporter* and National Public Radio (NPR).

Recognized as an expert in his field, Tom speaks regularly at national meetings, forums and universities about trends and opportunities in pharmaceutical sales, recruiting, motivation and leadership. He is a member of the American College of Healthcare Executives, U.S. Recruiters Organization and also serves as a consultant to the healthcare industry with the Gerson Lehrman Group. Tom now splits his time between Manhattan Beach, California, and New York City.

# Additional Tools and Resources

Please visit **www.tomruff.com** for additional information on Tom Ruff Company, and:

- Tom's Blog: **www.tomruff.com/blog**
- Industry news
- More interview questions and the psychology behind them
- Interview tips
- Sample résumé templates
- Helpful job search resources